THE

JAMES BEARD
FOUNDATION'S

Best of the Best

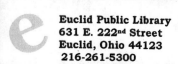

THE

JAMES BEARD
FOUNDATION'S

Best of the Best

A 25ᵀᴴ ANNIVERSARY CELEBRATION OF
AMERICA'S OUTSTANDING CHEFS

BY KIT WOHL

PHOTOGRAPHS BY SUSIE CUSHNER

FOREWORD BY MARTHA STEWART

CHRONICLE BOOKS

SAN FRANCISCO

IN MEMORY OF

Chef Robert Barker

MANUFACTURED IN China

DESIGNED BY Cat Grishaver

10 9 8 7 6 5 4 3 2 1

Chronicle Books LLC
680 Second Street
San Francisco, California 94107
www.chroniclebooks.com

CONTENTS

Foreword

MARTHA STEWART

Looking at the pictures and studying the recipes in this beautifully conceived, wonderfully photographed book, one gets an immediate sense of the scope, importance, and influence imposed on the American culinary taste by the many outstanding chefs who are featured. One also can understand more clearly how the "melting pot" that is America, the America that so thoroughly entranced the great James Beard with its incredible diversity and multiculturism, influenced the way these chefs cook.

There are twenty-one inspiring biographical monographs written by Kit Wohl about the twenty-one great chefs who have been selected as America's "Best of the Best." I was thrilled to realize that I have had each of these renowned chefs on my television shows. I have eaten their food more than once in my lifetime. And I know exactly why they were selected above all others as the "best": their talent as chefs, their acclaimed food, and their vast contributions to the American culinary landscape.

I remember every dish I ate at each of their restaurants, and the memories evoked by this book are lovely and deep. Each chef has been recognized for his or her contributions to the culinary traditions of America and for their originality, creativity, and individualism. Most are American, steeped in local culture but greatly devout in their belief that home grown and fresh is best and purity of ingredients essential for superior results, while others are European, or trained internationally.

How lucky we are to be the recipients of such wonderful recipes, all of which I plan to try in the very near future: Judy Rodgers' Zuni Bread Soup, Cavatelli with Pasta Enrico from Mario Batali, and even an intriguing dessert, the Limoncello Tiramisù, from Lidia Bastianich.

This book is not just a tribute to twenty-one great chefs and their histories. It is, most important, a book devoted to James Beard, a central figure in the acknowledgment and promotion of what we all nowadays call "American Cuisine." James Beard wrote more than thirty cookbooks, and he is credited with bringing French cooking to American cooks. He talked and gossiped and cooked his way through giant categories in the world of cuisine: breads, pasta, fish, barbecue, and casseroles, to name but a few.

I cherish many of his books, but my favorite is a tattered, worn-out first edition of *Beard on Bread* from 1973, which I still refer to for his Mother's Raisin Bread and a delectable Sally Lunn.

I remember meeting James Beard, a giant of a man with a large head, large hands, and a larger belly, at a foodie event hosted by Craig Claiborne and Pierre Franey. His jovial, loud, and boisterous personality was so awe inspiring, but even more so was the vastness of his knowledge, his collections of fine personal commentary, and recipes about the foods he was so passionate about.

The influence of James Beard is so widespread and his memory so very gracefully preserved, thanks to the James Beard Foundation, its good works, and the chefs and cooks everywhere who everyday practice what James Beard taught us so well.

introduction

SUSAN UNGARO, PRESIDENT OF THE JAMES BEARD FOUNDATION

with MITCHELL DAVIS, VICE PRESIDENT OF THE JAMES BEARD FOUNDATION

Looking back on the last 25 years, it's hard to believe how much American food and food culture has evolved. When the James Beard Foundation was founded in November 1986 by Peter Kump, Julia Child, and other friends and colleagues of James Beard, no one could have imagined that there would one day be two 24-hour television networks devoted to food programming and that just about every other station would have some sort of popular food content as well. Who could have conceived of anything like the Internet, let alone the hundreds of thousands of food blogs, the millions of people exchanging real-time information about restaurants and chefs and recipes and everything else? It would have been hard to envision a world where *Gourmet* magazine was electronic, just as it would have been impossible to think of using a mobile phone to search a recipe database to decide what to make for dinner.

At the center of all of this excitement and enthusiasm for food has been the chef. The original mission of the Beard Foundation was to shine a spotlight on the men and women who prepared the food we loved in celebrated restaurants, both new and old. The first chef to cook a dinner at the James Beard House was a young, dynamic Austrian chef from California named Wolfgang Puck whose restaurant Spago was wildly popular for inventive pizzas and other creative dishes. After Puck's dinner in January 1987, Peter Kump sent a thank-you letter noting that the success of his event gave the Foundation the idea of doing similar guest-chef benefit dinners monthly. In addition to providing a performance space for chefs from around the country and helping to raise money for the Foundation, Kump explained that these monthly dinners would be the start of a "tradition for showcasing new chefs who have not yet received recognition."(That would prove to be a prescient statement, as Puck went on to win the first award for Outstanding Chef that was given four years later and then in 1998 became the only chef to win the award twice.)

THE IMPORTANT ROLE OF CHEFS

As you make your way around the world's great food cultures, the chef doesn't always take center stage. Sure, French chefs are a prized part of France's cultural patrimony. But in Italy and Thailand, two great food cultures in their own right, big names in the kitchen are arguably less important than the food prepared in homes and local, casual eateries. Even in France, a rich regional food culture informs the palates of the populace before they sit down at the country's great tables. By contrast, in America, where our food culture has come to us top down—via experts such as James Beard and the chefs he inspired—and where the notion of celebrity is a byproduct of Hollywood, it was only a matter of time before the handsome men and women in starched white jackets and checked pants began to get their due.

By the end of 1990, the Beard Foundation's program calendar had expanded from one dinner per month to 15. In an article about a Beard Foundation event orchestrated by Oklahoma chef and Beard friend John Bennett, the *New York Times* called the Beard House "a shrine...where the nation's top culinary talent [are] showcased." Still, the Foundation's directors were looking for other ways to turn up their spotlight on American chefs. The James Beard Foundation Awards were born.

The James Beard Awards were formed in the fall of 1990 by combining two previously existing awards programs, one for books, one for food-world luminaries, and by creating a third program specifically designed to recognize the accomplishments of chefs and restaurateurs. The book awards began their life in 1966 as the R.T. French Tastemaker Awards. By the time the Beard Foundation assumed the administration of them, they were 25 years old and they had become the most prestigious awards for culinary books. Beard himself had won the Cookbook of the Year award in 1972 for *American Cookery*. The Who's Who of Cooking in America was established in 1985 by *Cooks* magazine. With the closing of *Cooks* in 1990, the Who's Who was also folded into the Beard Foundation Awards, where it was renamed the Who's Who of Food & Beverage in America.

AND THE WINNER IS...

But all eyes were on the new restaurant and chef awards. Without any restaurant-rating program that was national in scope and that carried the weight of, say, Michelin in France, Americans were left to local reviewers and the occasional one-off guidebook. Chefs, too, were hungry for the type of recognition afforded by a stringent, world-class, merit-based award system. (Michelin would not debut in America until 2006, when their first guide to New York City restaurants was released.) When the announcement of the Beard Foundation awards was made in December 1990, the *New York Times* deemed them to be an "important" development in the food world.

What made the Beard Awards unique was that the winners were not selected by a panel of experts, but by a jury of peers. Modeled after the Academy Awards—*Time* magazine would dub the Beard Awards the "Oscars of the food world" in 1992—the chef and restaurant winners were selected by a three-stage nomination and balloting process that has been only slightly modified since its inception. The process begins with an open call for entries during which anyone can suggest a favorite chef or restaurant. The top 20 to 30 entries in each category become the semifinalists. A panel of chefs and regional journalists then vote to narrow the semifinalists in each category down to five nominees. And then they vote on the nominees to pick the winner. Each year nominees and winners are added to the panel of judges who vote. The system helps identify chefs and other people working in the food world who might not have received national media attention but who are no less deserving of attention. The winner is announced at the awards ceremony, held each year on a Monday at the beginning of May, near James Beard's birthday, which was on May 5.

As soon as the first awards were given on May 6, 1991, at a ceremony aboard World Yacht's M.S. *New Yorker*, they changed the course of American food history. Then food editor of the *Los Angeles Times*, Ruth Reichl, devoted four full pages of text with color photographs (rare at the time) to her coverage of "the largest gathering of American chefs, restaurateurs, winemakers, and cookbook authors ever assembled in one place." Madeleine Kamman wrote in a letter to Peter Kump that "it took me a whole week to get over all these wonderful festivities." *New York Times* columnist Florence Fabricant called the event "a milestone in the food community."

Among the winners anointed at that first ceremony were Wolfgang Puck, who, as already mentioned, received the Outstanding Chef Award, Nancy Silverton, who won Outstanding Pastry Chef, and Bouley, which won Outstanding Restaurant. Also fêted were Best Chef: Mid-Atlantic Award winner Jean-Louis Palladin, who would go on to win the Outstanding Chef Award in 1993 and Best Chef: Midwest Award winner Rick Bayless, who would win Outstanding Chef in 1995. The first Lifetime Achievement award was given to M.F.K. Fisher.

Over the years, the James Beard Awards program has expanded into new areas, with Food Journalism, Broadcast and Electronic Media, Restaurant Design and Graphics all now part of the celebration. In addition to new awards programs, new awards categories have also been added over the years to reflect the changing landscape of restaurants, food, and chefs. The most up-to-date details are always available at www.jamesbeard.org/awards. Since 2007, the main chef and restaurant ceremony has made its home at the elegant Avery Fisher Hall at Lincoln Center. But because of the Beard Foundation's focus on chefs for more than a quarter century, the big moment of every year's awards ceremony is always the anointing of the Outstanding Chef.

A UNIQUELY AMERICAN CUISINE

"After sixty-five years I have come to the conclusion that perhaps American cookery is one of the most fascinating culinary subjects of all," wrote James Beard in the introduction to his chef d'oeuvre *American Cookery*. Much of his fascination came from the intermingling of different cultures, a hallmark of American society and of American cuisine. Although Beard certainly loved French cuisine and possessed a vast knowledge of Chinese food, he was ever intrigued by the literal melting pot that characterized our food. "I'm always asked what the dominating factor in American cuisine is," Beard wrote in an article about the American attitude toward food that was published in 1983. "And my reply is that it's the many ethnic groups, each of which brought its own ideas of food to this country."

Flipping through the pages of this beautiful collection of recipes and reading the biographical sketches of winners of the James Beard Outstanding Chef Award through the years, you see clearly that the culinary multiculturalism Beard deemed so integral to American cooking continues to inform the country's best chefs. Whether it is Wolfgang Puck's Austrian upbringing, the Mexican traditions that inspire Rick and Deann Bayless, Lidia Bastianich's and Mario Batali's Italian heritage, or the Thai flavors that perfume

Jean-Georges Vongerichten's Alsatian cooking, American chefs have forged a unique approach to food that draws on the ingredients and techniques of the entire world. And American diners continue to want our chefs to push the boundaries and the boldness farther.

This openness to and enthusiasm for crossing boundaries make American cuisine unique and exciting. Chefs from Europe and Asia come to our kitchens to learn how to integrate various traditions into a cohesive style of cooking. Certainly any chef is well served by studying Italian food in Italy and Japanese food in Japan. But to study how to blend the two into a cuisine that moves beyond the traditions of either one, for that sort of education they have to come to America.

The same openness and enthusiasm are also what make American cuisine so difficult to define. In 2007 the James Beard Foundation hosted a national food festival called Taste America in 20 cities across the country. As part of the festivities we conducted a national online survey about American cuisine, asking participants to try to define it and to name iconic American dishes. Not surprisingly, the definitions were loose. Regional, local, melting pot, and other terms seasoned the answers, but no clear idea of what American cuisine is emerged. By contrast, survey respondents were certain about what the most iconic foods were (in order of popularity): hamburgers, barbecue, fried chicken, macaroni and cheese, and apple pie.

What's interesting is that none of these iconic American dishes appear in the pages of this book of iconic American chefs. Interesting, but not surprising. Certainly any one of these chefs would know how to make a delicious burger or fry up a crisp piece of chicken. And most of them have probably had some form of macaroni and cheese on their menu at one time or another. While these dishes are not included here, somehow they aren't that far in the background. The bold, straightforward cheesiness of a good mac'n'cheese, the simple, eat-with-your-hands casualness of burgers and fried chicken are still part of our gastronomic makeup, even when we are sitting down to an elegant multicourse dégustation. The universal appeal of these iconic dishes helps alleviate the pretentiousness that can often accompany cooking at the culinary heights these Outstanding Chefs inhabit. "I sometimes wonder if my being just one generation from the covered wagon makes me feel so allied to this country's gastronomic treasures," Beard wrote. Well, perhaps none of us is that far away.

James Beard wrote more than 25 cookbooks in his lifetime, so it is fitting to celebrate the 25th anniversary of the Foundation that bears his name with this incredibly beautiful book. We are grateful to all of the Outstanding Chefs who contributed their time and talent as well as to the thousands of chefs who have passed through James Beard's kitchen since Wolfgang Puck first gave us the idea that showcasing American chefs might be a noble mission for the Foundation to pursue. The world of cuisine is ever grateful to those who had the vision to make the James Beard Foundation a reality and to those who will carry on James Beard's legacy of a bona fide American cuisine into the future. Today our mission reads, "To celebrate, nurture, and preserve America's diverse culinary heritage and future." By supporting the men and women who make great food and who inspire us to cook, we are all helping to fulfill that mission.

In 2008, Deborah Soloman in the *New York Times Magazine* asked American poet laureate Charles Simic, "What advice would you give to people who are looking to be happy?"

"For starters," Simic answered, "learn how to cook."

EDITOR'S NOTE:

As we went to press, José Andrés was honored with the 2011 James Beard Outstanding Chef Award for his exceptional talent and successful restaurants, most notably minibar by José Andrés and Jaleo in Washington, D.C. Chef Andrés, who has become known for popularizing tapas and contemporary Spanish cuisine in America and for mixing food and politics, said, "Food is the most powerful thing we have in our hands. Not only for chefs, but everyone in the food community. The right use of food can end hunger."

1991 & 1998

WOLFGANG PUCK

CHAPTER *one*

WOLFGANG PUCK'S NAME MAY NOW EVOKE FOR MANY PEOPLE VISIONS OF HOLLYWOOD GLAMOUR, OF AMERICA'S FIRST REAL "CELEBRITY CHEF." But Spago, the restaurant that catapulted Puck to stardom, was never originally intended to be a particularly fancy or glamorous place.

Ask Puck today why Spago became such a success, and his first instinct is to deflect the credit to Hollywood itself. "'Swifty' Lazar, Orson Welles, they made it famous," he says, letting their names stand in for the throngs of Tinseltown powers who began flocking to Spago when it first opened in an unassuming location above the Sunset Strip in 1982.

Spago's success was based on more than just being a celebrity hangout, or on the gourmet pizza that won so much attention in the early days. Spago pioneered many restaurant concepts taken for granted in restaurants today: the "open kitchen,"—in Puck's case, a wood-burning pizza oven—became part of the dining excitement; an emphasis on cooking with locally produced, in-season ingredients; and the notion that "fine" dining didn't have to be a stuffy, formal experience but could instead be casual, relaxed, and fun. He was also a serious chef, possessing a lifetime of personal and top professional cooking experiences when he opened Spago at the age of thirty-two.

Puck grew up far from ostentation in a cottage with no television or radio in Sankt Veit an der Glan, a tiny village in southern Austria. He first learned cooking from his grandmother and his mother, Maria Puck, who was pastry chef and baker at the Hotel Linde in the lakeside resort town of Maria Wörth. "I used to go there with her every summer," Puck remembers, "and I would follow the chefs around. Against the wishes of my father, who thought cooking was not a man's job, I decided I wanted to become a pastry chef. But I couldn't find an apprenticeship."

When Puck was fourteen, the owner of the Hotel Linde found him an entry-level job at the Hotel Post in Villach. But the chef there didn't like his work and fired him after a month. Despondent and not wanting to go home a failure, the teenager sneaked back into the kitchen. With the aid of another cook, he hid and slept in the root cellar, peeling potatoes for his keep. The hotel's owner discovered him weeks later and found the persistent Puck another job at the Park Hotel. "I spent three years there, completing my apprenticeship, getting my certificate as a chef, and finishing first in my age group in a national culinary competition when I was sixteen."

Puck moved on as part of the kitchen team at Aux Trois Faisans in Dijon, France. "After a year, I found out I'd been working in a Michelin one-star restaurant," Puck says. "Then, I saw that some other restaurants had two and three stars, so I wrote to them asking for work."

Even though the legendary Paul Bocuse was among the chefs to whom Puck sent those letters, his response came from the great Raymond Thuillier, chef of L'Oustau de Baumanière in Les Baux, which is considered the three-star pinnacle of Provençal cuisine. "Thuillier was my mentor," Puck says. "I spent two-and-a-half years there and saw what it meant to be a chef doing your own style of cooking. Thuillier had only started to cook professionally when he was around fifty, so he didn't have the rigidity of many men his age in the kitchen. I really started to understand the potential that food had, and it was the first time I started to really like cooking. We used only fresh vegetables and everything was cooked to order. That's still how I believe a restaurant must work."

From there, Puck cooked in Paris for a while before heading back south to the two-star La Reserve in Beaulieu, where he served briefly as a *chef de partis* (line cook)—"very elegant, but run like an army." He left the country for lack of a green card leading to to a stint at the Hotel de Paris in Monte Carlo, where he was the number-one commis, or assistant chef, on the vegetable station. Puck's return to France was his "next big jump up" as *chef de partis* at the historic Maxim's in Paris, cooking a modernized style of classic French cuisine. Promoted to night chef, it was a lively time when guests included Brigitte Bardot, Jeanne Moreau, Sylvie Vartan, and Barbra Streisand.

Puck became executive chef at La Tour in Indianapolis, Indiana, a job that appealed to him not only as his stepping stone to America but also as a fan of car racing, fueled by his time in Monte

Carlo. He admits that his approach was too revved-up for his first job as head of a restaurant kitchen. "I was so hyper then," he recalls. "I screamed and yelled constantly." He soon realized, however, that doing so wasn't the most productive way to manage an American kitchen brigade.

A year later, drawn by the excitement and opportunities of the West Coast, he moved to his employer's Los Angeles restaurant. Puck soon met restaurateur Patrick Terrail, whose Uncle Claude owned the four-century-old Tour d'Argent in Paris. Terrail had opened a bistro called Ma Maison, where Puck started cooking part-time. He quickly took over the kitchen, and, by June 1975, Puck became the co-owner. Both his cooking and his boyish charm soon had a following of Hollywood royalty like Billy Wilder, Jack Lemmon, and Orson Welles, who especially enjoyed sharing a glass of Mumm de Cramant Grand Cru Champagne with the likeable young chef to kick off lunch every day.

After six years at Ma Maison, Puck decided to open his own place, and so he ended the partnership with Terrail on July 4, 1981. "That was my Independence Day."

For his new restaurant, he settled on the name *Spago*, Mediterranean slang for "spaghetti," which had been suggested by Italian songwriter, producer, and recording artist Giorgio Moroder. "He was supposed to be the main investor for the restaurant and said that the name would be perfect because it also poetically referred to a string that never ends," Puck explains. "Morodoer never wound up giving us the money, but the name stuck anyway."

There was more to the Spago concept than the name. "I thought that Southern California reminded me of the Riviera or, even more, of Italy's Amalfi coast. Yet, at the time, people in the city still had the idea that fine dining meant eating in a formal French restaurant with starched white tablecloths and waiters in tuxedos." He set out to change the definition of a great meal. "I decided that rather than serving the kind of dishes you might get in Paris or Lyon, I wanted to grill food to order over oak wood or vine trimmings, like they did in the Mediterranean, without complicated sauces, and

to keep everything simple." He had also recently seen a wood-fired pizza oven in a pizzeria where a friend was working. "I thought that would be a fun thing to have in an upscale restaurant."

Spago, which was designed by Puck's former wife Barbara Lazaroff, opened on January 16, 1982. They furnished the restaurant on a tight budget, with patio tables and chairs. "People smiled when they saw it and they immediately felt relaxed," Puck says. "All these people who were used to stuffy restaurants got the joke." But the food, though casual, was no joke; Puck concentrated on using the best ingredients he could find. "At that time, people were used to ordering fresh tomato salads all year round," Puck says. "But we would not sell a tomato salad in the wintertime." He was the first non-Asian chef to frequent the Japanese fish market for his seafood. He brought in the best fresh sand dabs from Monterey. A farmer in Sonoma raised lamb especially to Puck's specifications. He went to Chinatown to buy his chickens—and also bought a Chinese smoker to tea-smoke his ducks. Soon, Puck had cultivated a relationship that continues to this day with Chino Farm, considered one of the region's finest sources for seasonal vegetables and fruits. "The only thing completely serious at Spago was what was on the plate."

Puck's pizzas grabbed media attention and customer devotion. He didn't invent the idea of a crispy, cracker-thin crust, but that was just the sort that suited his light, inventive, California-style approach. His toppings introduced delicious new possibilities in savory pies: goat cheese, pesto, sun-dried tomatoes, fresh Santa Barbara shrimp, truffles, and fresh sausage made with the meat from those Sonoma lambs.

Not long after Spago had opened, he created one of its most famous pizzas as a last-minute act of whimsy. The actress Joan Collins had come in for a late dinner and ordered an appetizer of their house-smoked salmon. "We always served it traditional style, with toasted brioche, chopped sweet onion, capers, chives, and lemon wedges," Puck recalls. "But that night, we were so busy that we ran out of brioche, so I rolled out some pizza dough to give her instead. At the last minute, though, I decided to cover the hot-from-the-oven pizza dough with some crème fraîche flavored with fresh dill, add some onions, draped the smoked salmon on top, and, because Joan loved caviar, put a big dollop of that in the center. Other guests started demanding it as soon as they saw it on the way to Joan's table."

Spago's smoked salmon pizza became an instant sensation. He gradually began building an empire of other restaurants and branded activities. Chinois on Main, his second restaurant, opened in Santa Monica in 1983 and kicked off fusion cuisine—another major food trend. The menu, from Puck and Ma Maison and Spago alumnus Kazuto Matsusaka, melded Chinese, Japanese, Thai, and Korean influences with the chef's Californian and French training, and was served in a dining room created by Lazaroff as a bold fantasia of Asian design. After that came Postrio, located in San Francisco's Prescott Hotel. In 1992, Puck became the first name-brand chef to open a restaurant in Las Vegas with Spago in The Forum Shops at Caesars Palace. Five more restaurants followed at various locations.

Today, Puck has two dozen fine-dining restaurants; including Spago in Beverly Hills, Las Vegas, Maui, and Beaver Creek, Colorado; Chinois and his new ultra-elegant pan-Asian WP24, which opened in 2010 in the Ritz-Carlton in Los Angeles; and additional establishments in Singapore, Detroit, Minneapolis, Dallas, Atlantic City, and Washington, D.C. The elegant steakhouse CUT, an acclaimed new concept, debuted in the Beverly Wilshire Hotel in 2006, and now boasts three locations, with a fourth slated to open in London in 2011. And then there are multiple locations of the quick-casual Wolfgang Puck Express and Wolfgang Puck Bistro. Five million fresh and frozen Wolfgang Puck pizzas sold each year; twenty-six varieties of Wolfgang Puck canned soup are licensed to Campbell's; and Wolfgang Puck-branded cookware, small appliances, kitchen accessories, and tableware are sold on HSN.

Puck seems at times to be everywhere at once. His frequent appearances on ABC's *Good Morning America* have made him a regular since 1986. He hosted an Emmy Award–winning Food Network series in the early 2000s and is the author of six cookbooks.

How does he do it all and still maintain the level of quality and creativity for which he is renowned? Credit some of that success to the fact that he has mentored some of the most talented cooks in America, including Mark Peel, Nancy Silverton, Neal Fraser, Govind Armstrong, Michael Cimarusti, Josiah Citrin, and Quinn and Karen Hatfield, as well as Spago executive chef and corporate managing partner Lee Hefter, and executive pastry chef Sherry Yard.

"I'VE LEARNED THAT TO BE A SUCCESS AT ANYTHING," HE SAYS, "YOU'VE GOT TO FIND THE BEST PEOPLE, TRAIN THEM WELL, LET THEM KNOW WHAT YOU EXPECT, TREAT THEM WELL, AND THEN ALLOW THEM THE FREEDOM TO DO WHAT THEY DO BEST."

Puck has the seemingly boundless energy of a man who truly loves what he does. On weekdays, he can be found at Spago Beverly Hills. He is constantly on the move between the kitchen, working alongside his chefs, and the dining room, stopping by at tables and greeting guests. He cheerfully poses for photos and autographs cookbooks. Later he drives to Chinois or WP24 to make the same rounds. "By the time I get home, it can be after midnight," he admits. "But I tell everyone that twelve hours is only half a day. If you only work twelve hours, you're never going to be successful." On weekends, he may be participating in philanthropic activities, and Puck relishes time with older sons Cameron and Byron, and family life with his wife, Gelila, and their two young sons, Oliver and Alexander.

The first James Beard Foundation Outstanding Chef honoree—and the only person to be awarded that honor twice—played a major role in the California culinary revolution, and has turned into an American celebration of health-conscious, sustainable, and delicious dining habits. He has done it all by following a recipe for success that is disarming in its directness and modesty: "Do what you love. Work hard. Be patient. And, with a little luck, you could succeed."

LOBSTER SHANGHAI STYLE *with* CRISPY SPINACH

1 piece fresh ginger, approximately 1 inch

2 garlic cloves, minced

¾ cup plum wine or port, divided

2 tablespoons rice vinegar

2 tablespoons peanut oil

One 2-pound lobster, split lengthwise

2 tablespoons unsalted butter, divided

4 scallions, cut into ⅜-inch slices

1 to 2 teaspoons curry powder

½ cup fish stock

¼ cup dry white wine

1 tablespoon Chinese black vinegar or balsamic vinegar

½ teaspoon dried hot chili flakes

½ cup heavy cream

Salt

Freshly ground black pepper

12 large spinach leaves

Peanut oil, for frying

1. Preheat the oven to 500°F.

2. Peel the ginger, reserving the peels, and cut it into thin strips. Cut the peels into coarse strips. In a small saucepan, cook the ginger and garlic with ½ cup of the plum wine and the rice wine vinegar until 1 tablespoon of liquid remains. Remove from the heat.

3. Place a heavy, heatproof 12-inch skillet over high heat. Add the oil, then carefully add the lobster halves, meat-side down. Cook for 3 minutes. Turn the lobsters over and add 1 tablespoon of the butter. Continue to sauté until the lobster shells get red and the butter is nutty red. Transfer the lobsters to the oven for about 10 minutes, or until the meat is just cooked. Remove from the oven, remove the lobsters from the skillet, and keep warm.

4. Add the scallions, ginger peels, and curry powder to the skillet. Over high heat, sauté the mixture for 10 to 15 seconds, then whisk in the remaining plum wine, stock, white wine, black vinegar, and chili flakes. Reduce the liquid to ½ cup. Add the cream and reduce it by half. Add any liquid from the julienne of ginger, then whisk in the remaining 1 tablespoon butter. Season the sauce with salt and pepper.

5. Wash the spinach, cut off the stems, and dry the leaves well. In a large pot, heat the oil to 375°F and fry the spinach until crisp. Remove to paper towels to drain. Salt lightly.

6. Crack the lobster claws with the back of a large chef's knife. Arrange the lobster halves on a warm platter, meat-side down. Strain the sauce over the lobster, then sprinkle the sweet ginger on top. Garnish with the spinach leaves.

SERVES 2

PIZZA *with* SMOKED SALMON *and* CAVIAR

PIZZA DOUGH

2½ teaspoons active dry yeast

1 teaspoon honey

1 cup warm water (105 to 115°F), divided

3 cups all-purpose flour,
plus additional for stretching the dough

1 teaspoon kosher salt

1 tablespoon extra-virgin olive oil,
plus additional for brushing

TOPPINGS

¼ cup extra-virgin olive oil

1 medium red onion, cut into julienne strips

2 tablespoons minced fresh dill,
plus 4 small sprigs for garnish

1 cup sour cream or crème fraîche

Freshly ground black pepper

1 pound smoked salmon, sliced paper thin

4 heaping tablespoons domestic golden caviar

4 heaping teaspoons black caviar

1. In a small bowl, dissolve the yeast and honey in ¹/₄ cup of the warm water.

2. In a mixer fitted with a dough hook, combine the flour and salt. Add the oil, yeast mixture, and the remaining 3/4 cup water and mix on low speed until the dough comes cleanly away from the sides of the bowl and clusters around the dough hook, about 5 minutes. (The pizza dough can also be made in a food processor. Dissolve the yeast as above. Combine the flour and salt in the bowl of a food processor fitted with the metal blade. Pulse once or twice, add the remaining ingredients, and process until the dough begins to form a ball that rides around the side of the bowl on top of the blade.)

3. Turn the dough out onto a clean work surface and knead by hand 2 or 3 minutes longer. The dough should feel smooth and firm. Cover the dough with a clean, damp towel and let it rise in a warm spot for about 30 minutes. When ready, the dough should stretch easily as it is lightly pulled.

4. Place a pizza stone on the middle rack of the oven and preheat it to 500°F.

CONTINUED

5. Divide the dough into 4 balls, about 6 ounces each. Work each ball by pulling down the sides and tucking under the bottom of the ball. Repeat four or five times to form a smooth, even, firm ball. Then on a smooth, unfloured surface, roll the ball under the palm of your hand until the top of the dough is smooth and firm, about 1 minute. Cover the dough with a damp towel and let it rest 15 to 20 minutes. At this point, the balls can be wrapped in plastic and refrigerated for up to 2 days.

6. To prepare each pizza, dip a ball of dough into flour, shake off the excess flour, place the dough on a clean, lightly floured surface, and start to stretch the dough. While turning it, press down on the center with the heel of your hand, spreading the dough into an 8-inch circle, with its outer rim a little thicker than the inner circle. If you find this difficult to do, use a small rolling pin to roll out the dough.

7. Place the pizza on a lightly floured pizza peel or rimless baking sheet. Brush the center of the pizza to within 1 inch of the edge with the olive oil and sprinkle it with some of the onion. Slide the pizza onto the baking stone and bake 8 to 12 minutes, or until the crust is golden brown. Carefully remove the pizza with the peel or baking sheet and transfer it to a cutting board.

8. Mix the dill with the sour cream or crème fraîche and season with pepper. Transfer the pizza to a heated dinner plate and spread it with ¼ cup of the sour cream mixture.

9. Divide the salmon into 4 portions, and arrange one portion decoratively over the cream.

10. Place a spoonful of golden caviar in the center of the pizza, then spoon a little of the black caviar into the center of the golden caviar. With a pizza cutter or large, sharp knife, cut the pizza into fourths and serve immediately. Repeat with the remaining dough and toppings for 3 more pizzas.

SERVES 4

KAISERSCHMARRN

STRAWBERRY SAUCE

8 ounces organic strawberries, hulled

1/2 orange, juiced

1/4 cup dry white wine

3 tablespoons sugar

1 1/2 teaspoons orange zest

1 1/2 teaspoons fresh lemon juice

1/2 whole star anise

KAISER BASE

3 large eggs, separated

1 large egg yolk

2/3 cup sugar, plus extra for garnish

8 ounces crème fraîche

2 tablespoons dark rum

2 tablespoons plumped organic golden raisins

4 teaspoons flour

Unsalted butter, at room temperature, for brushing

1 pound organic strawberries, hulled and halved

1. Combine all the ingredients for the strawberry sauce in a medium saucepan. Bring to a boil. Cook for 5 minutes. Remove from the heat and cover with plastic wrap. Allow the flavors to infuse for 10 minutes. Transfer the mixture to a blender and process until well incorporated. Strain. The sauce can be prepared up to 3 days ahead and refrigerated.

2. To make the kaiser base, in the bowl of a stand mixer fitted with the whisk attachment, combine the egg yolks and about 1/2 cup of the sugar. Mix on medium speed until pale yellow. Add the crème fraîche and rum. Continue to mix until smooth. Fold in the raisins and flour. The base can be prepared up to 1 day in advance and refrigerated.

3. Preheat the oven to 425°F. Brush four 6-inch sauté pans with butter and sprinkle with sugar.

4. In a clean bowl, whisk the egg whites to soft peaks. Add the remaining sugar and continue to whip until stiff but not dry. Fold the meringue into the kaiser base. Spoon the mixture into the 4 pans. Bake until golden brown and nicely risen, about 12 minutes.

5. In a medium sauté pan, reheat the strawberry sauce. Add the fresh strawberries and toss until well coated. Divide among individual plates. Spoon kaiserschmarrn over the berries and serve immediately.

SERVES 4 TO 8

1992

ALICE WATERS

CHAPTER *two*

IT'S BEEN ALMOST FORTY YEARS SINCE ALICE WATERS GAVE A RAMSHACKLE HOUSE IN BERKELEY, CALIFORNIA, A FRESH START AS A RESTAURANT, GROWING IT INTO A BEACON OF ORGANIC, SUSTAINABLE EATING. Waters herself has become widely recognized as one of the foremost voices in reshaping the way Americans view food.

Waters wasn't thinking about organic food or sustainable agriculture or including farmers in a "movement" when she persuaded a group of friends to invest in a French-style neighborhood bistro in 1971. The twenty-seven-year-old had never even worked in a restaurant, but she thought Chez Panisse could serve delightful meals and be an informal gathering place for good food and enlightened conversation.

From the beginning, her goal was to recreate the flavors and community that she experienced during a sojourn in France in the mid-1960s. There, she was particularly impressed by the taste of food and the numerous farmers' markets where people bought fresh produce daily and cooked it in their homes that same day. She took note of a culture where everyone, it seemed, enjoyed food— buying it, preparing it, eating it, and sharing it with friends and family. Thus Waters positioned herself more as proprietress of Chez Panisse: meeting, greeting, and mingling, and serving as the establishment's authority on taste.

The restaurant was named for Honoré Panisse, the generous and life-loving character in Marcel Pagnol's 1930s Fanny Trilogy of films ("Marius," "Fanny," and "César"). The restaurant's name was an homage to the warmth, comedy, and informality of the classic films.

Waters graduated in 1967 from the University of California, Berkeley, where free speech, women's rights, and the student anti-war movement honed her idealistic perspective. She tried to right what she believed was wrong, without concern for consequence. Her activist nature became entrenched during that time.

Through its first decade, the restaurant had dramatic ups and downs, but Waters kept her eye on her goal, and when the ingredients like those she relished in France were unavailable from the usual purveyors, she convinced local farmers to grow seasonal produce that would be cooked as soon after harvest as possible.

Consequently, she helped stimulate a community of local farmers, ranchers, and fisherman who assured a steady supply of ingredients. Waters also began to educate herself about organic farming. Soon, she was swept up in, often leading, the emerging California culinary revolution of the 1970s and 1980s that ushered in local, organically grown foods, a trend that was nurtured by California's chefs and vintners.

In the 1970s, with Waters as proprietor and Jeremiah Tower as chef, the two presented regionally themed French menus made with California's bounty. The trend that celebrated local ranchers, fishermen, and farmers began emerging in other parts of the country, inspired by what was happening on the West Coast.

Waters has also been a pioneer in promoting education about food production, the benefits of good nutrition, and respect for the environment. As she has influenced the American culinary scene, Chez Panisse has continued to gain national recognition and honors. Waters feels that good food should be a right and not a privilege; that meats should be antibiotic and hormone free; that produce should be grown without pesticides and herbicides. She believes that everyone deserves this food and that this approach is not elitist.

Waters was awarded the French Legion of Honor in April 2010 in recognition of her success in preserving and bringing to America French food values and traditions. Rarely given to a chef, the honor really touched Waters. "I realized that I was preserving a lot more than just my own taste and way of doing it and running a restaurant.

I WAS FEEDING BACK RIGHT INTO THAT RIVER OF HUMANITY THAT CHERISHES THE VALUES OF SUSTAINABILITY, FRIENDSHIP, GENEROSITY, AND ALL THOSE THINGS THAT HAVE BEEN PART OF CIVILIZATION SINCE THE BEGINNING OF TIME."

Chez Panisse reflects Waters's desire for relaxed dining in a low-key, hospitable atmosphere. The set menu changes every night, appropriate to the season, featuring the finest local organic ingredients. Monday night's menus are simpler than other evenings; Friday's and Saturday's menus are more complex and more expensive.

In 1980, the Café at Chez Panisse opened upstairs from the iconic restaurant. The Café offers a casual alternative to the formal downstairs menu, serving a moderately priced à la carte menu inspired by the daily market. The open kitchen along one side of the room showcases a wood-burning oven that has been a fixture in the restaurant almost from the beginning. It is now paired with a charcoal grill.

The classic Craftsman style of the building has been maintained, with flourishes of casually arranged colorful fruits, vegetables, and flowers. Each spring, bursts of white and purple wisteria blooms dress the outside of the building, setting a beautiful stage for the food within.

As testament to Waters's pioneering spirit and culinary vision, numerous well-known chefs have worked at Chez Panisse on their way up, to absorb the fundamental ethics of the restaurant, among them Mark Miller, Jonathan Waxman, and Judy Rodgers (named Outstanding Chef 2004 by the James Beard Foundation), who began her career there as the lunch chef. Gilbert Pilgram, Rodgers's partner at her restaurant, Zuni Café, was himself a mainstay at Chez Panisse for twenty-five years before he retired, then went back into the business with Rodgers.

Rodgers, who spent a summer in France with the culinary Troisgros family, says the fact that Michel Troisgros, the son of Pierre Troisgros, worked at Chez Panisse from 1978 to 1980, made a statement about the potential of the restaurant and the direction of food in America at that time. "It was pretty amazing that the Troisgros family would send their son to work in this little restaurant in San Francisco, because that was an era when you sent them to apprentice with Michel Guérard and Roger Vergé," Rodgers commented. The Troisgros family understood that the American market was important, she says, "But I also think it was partly their sense of adventure—they sensed that Chez Panisse was an important direction for food."

In 1996, long before better food in school lunches became a national issue, Waters embarked on a mission to teach children about healthy eating and respect for the environment with a gardening and cooking project she labeled Edible Schoolyard.

Through the Chez Panisse Foundation, an organization created by Waters to support programs that bring healthy food and eating into schools, the first garden and kitchen-classroom was established at the Martin Luther King Jr. Middle School in Berkeley. Students grow, harvest, and prepare food on the site, which teaches them to appreciate how food is produced and prepared, and in turn, encourages them to eat healthier foods. As Waters says, "This is an effort to bring kids into a new relationship to food; not telling children what they should eat, just allowing them to fall in love with nature and with culture. And it's not hard because they have been starved of good food for so long."

Waters enthusiastically advocates creating a curriculum that teaches food principles, from growing fruits and vegetables to harvesting and cooking them, in every public school in America. The Chez Panisse Foundation provides a precise blueprint and guideline for planning and implementing the program; its thoroughness is inspired by Waters's training at a Montessori school following college. Edible Schoolyards have been planted and are growing in urban acres across the country and more are being planned. Waters wrote recently, "The schools must become the places where we teach our children slow-food values. There should be gardens in every school, and there should be school lunch programs that serve real food, local, sustainably grown food."

Waters particularly admires Michelle Obama for her commitment to food education by involving children in the White House's organic garden and her work to bring better food to the nation's schools. "Seeds for the Future" would be an appropriate headline for the culinary garden at the White House, suggests Waters. "What's so important is that Michelle Obama really grew up with a set of values that included this big ecological picture, and obviously her love for children and their good health," she says. The First Lady, by speaking from her heart, has made better nutrition her own cause, Waters notes. "I'd like to think that I shoveled in some fertile soil there. But she made it her own, and I was just thrilled that she brought in school children—thrilled that it happened two months after Obama got into office. They even have a beehive and a compost heap."

Food activist Poppy Tooker, founder of Slow Food New Orleans, who helped spur an Edible Schoolyard project in that city, says of Waters, "Alice is completely uncompromising, and with her extreme standards in the food world, is able to carry it all off with an enchanting sweet smile." Tooker warns the unwary, "Waters carries a sledgehammer of determination. Given her way—and she'll probably get it—every child in America will eat real food. And she'll make it possible for children from kindergarten all the way to high school to be educated about ecology and gastronomy. Alice's incredible, driving will is more than anyone else I've ever come across."

Waters has always believed that ideas about healthy food have to be stamped in important places. Through Slow Food Nation, a branch of the Slow Food movement, gardens for the public's viewing were planted in front of City Hall in San Francisco and on the Mall in Washington, D.C., as part of a Smithsonian event.

During a Los Angeles conference in 2010, Waters emphasized projects that have inspired her, such as the Greensborough Children's Museum in North Carolina that allows children to grow food in the garden and also shop for vegetables in a store that is part of the museum. "The idea of linking food with art and culture is terribly important," Waters says. "Not just agriculture—that's vital—but to bring food back into the beauty of a museum just kind of takes my breath away. It's where I'm trying to go right now. Out of the place of foodies and into the place of tradition and ritual."

She points to the two-day garden installed in 2010 at the Arc de Triomphe in Paris extending down to the Place de la Concorde, as the most spectacular example of creating beauty with food. More than 8,000 plots of earth, 150,000 plants, and almost 700 fully grown trees as well as pigs, cows, horses, and sheep were on display. The purpose was to educate visitors and demonstrate the values of Mother Nature by highlighting her work. Waters sees boundless possibilities for other such gardens in many other places: "It's these kinds of ideas that can lift our spirits right now, and we need to hear about the good news."

SUMMER SALAD *garden lettuce salad*

ADAPTED FROM *THE ART OF SIMPLE FOOD*

1 garlic clove, peeled

1 tablespoon red wine vinegar

Salt

Freshly ground black pepper

¼ cup extra-virgin olive oil

4 handfuls mixed greens (8 ounces)

3 radishes, sliced into rounds

1 tablespoon coarsely chopped fresh chives or chervil

1. With a mortar and pestle, purée the garlic. Transfer the garlic to a bowl, add the vinegar, and season with salt and pepper. Whisk in the oil to make a vinaigrette.

2. In a large bowl, add the greens, radishes, chives or chervil, or both.

3. Add three-quarters of the vinaigrette; toss, and taste. Add more dressing as needed. Serve immediately.

SERVES 4

TURNIP *and* TURNIP GREENS SOUP

FROM *CHEZ PANISSE VEGETABLES*

2½ pounds young turnips with greens, washed

1 tablespoon olive oil

1 tablespoon unsalted butter

1 yellow onion, thinly sliced

1 garlic clove, thinly sliced

2 quarts chicken stock

2 ounces prosciutto or smoked bacon, diced

1 bay leaf

½ teaspoon chopped fresh thyme

Salt

Freshly ground black pepper

Extra-virgin olive oil, for garnish

Parmesan cheese, grated, for garnish (optional)

1. Trim the turnips, reserving the leaves. Peel the turnips unless very small and tender. Cut them crosswise into thin slices and reserve.

2. In a nonreactive saucepan over low to medium heat, combine the oil, butter, and 1 table-spoon water. Add the onion and garlic. Sauté until translucent. Add the turnips and cook until soft, approximately 4 minutes. Add the stock, prosciutto, bay leaf, thyme, and season with salt and pepper. Cover and simmer over low heat until the turnips are very tender, about 1 hour. Working in batches in a blender or food processor, purée the mixture until smooth.

3. Bring a small stockpot or large saucepan two-thirds full of salted water to a rolling boil. Blanch the turnip greens by boiling until tender, about 30 seconds; immediately plunge them into ice water. The leaves should be tender but still bright green. Purée the greens with a little of the soup.

4. Ladle the soup into serving bowls. Drizzle the blended turnip greens on top, drizzle with extra-virgin olive oil, and garnish with Parmesan, if using.

NOTE: Water or vegetable stock may be substituted for the chicken stock and the prosciutto omitted for a meatless version of this soup.

SERVES 4 TO 6

APRICOT GALETTE

ADAPTED FROM *CHEZ PANISSE FRUIT*

GALETTE DOUGH

2 cups unbleached all-purpose flour

1 teaspoon sugar

¼ teaspoon salt

¾ cup unsalted butter, chilled, diced ½ inch

7 tablespoons ice water

FRANGIPANE

1 cup almond paste

½ cup unsalted butter, at room temperature

1 large egg

2 tablespoons sugar

3 teaspoons flour

GALETTE

Flour for dusting

3 pounds ripe apricots, pitted and quartered

1 cup plus ¼ cup sugar, divided

2 tablespoons unsalted butter, melted

To make the galette dough

1. Combine the flour, sugar, and salt in a large mixing bowl. Cut ¼ cup of the butter into the flour mixture with a pastry blender, mixing until the mixture resembles coarse corn-meal. Cut in the remaining butter with the pastry blender until the mixture again resembles coarse cornmeal. Sprinkle the ice water into the flour mixture gradually, tossing and mixing between additions, until the dough just holds together. Continue tossing until it is ropy with some dry patches. If it's too dry, add an additional tablespoon of water and toss until the dough comes together. Do not overwork the dough.

CONTINUED

2. Divide the dough in half; firmly press each half into a ball. Wrap tightly in plastic wrap. Press down, flattening each ball into a 4-inch disk. Refrigerate for at least 30 minutes before rolling out. (Store the remaining dough in the refrigerator up to 2 days.)

3. When the dough is malleable but still cold, place 1 disk on a lightly floured surface and roll it into a 14-inch circle 1/8 inch thick. Remove excess flour from both sides with a dry pastry brush. Transfer the dough to an upside-down baking sheet lined with parchment and refrigerate for at least 30 minutes before using.

To make the frangipane

1. In a small bowl, mix the almond paste and butter until smooth. Add the egg, sugar, and flour and combine well. Reserve.

To make the galette

1. Put a pizza stone on the lower rack and preheat the oven to 400°F. Spread 1/4 cup of the frangipane on the dough round and dust it lightly with flour. Leaving the border bare, layer the apricots, skin-side down, and snugly touching, in concentric circles on the dough. Evenly sprinkle 1/2 cup of the sugar over the apricots. While rotating, fold and crimp the exposed dough edge against the outer circle of fruit. Fold the dough edge up and over itself at regular intervals, creating a containing rim resembling a length of rope. Pinch off any excess dough. Brush the crust edge with melted butter and sprinkle with the remaining 2 tablespoons sugar.

2. Slide the parchment paper and dough onto the pizza stone. Bake until the crust is well browned and the edges are slightly caramelized, 45 to 50 minutes. Remove from the oven and immediately place the galette on a cooling rack. Cool for 20 minutes before slicing.

SERVES 8

1993

LARRY FORGIONE

CHAPTER *three*

"IF JAMES BEARD IS KNOWN AS THE 'FATHER' OF AMERICAN CUISINE, THEN LARRY FORGIONE IS CERTAINLY THE 'GOD-FATHER,'" according to John Mariani, author, critic, and food authority, who assigned the moniker decades ago, explaining that, "Larry Forgione followed Beard's inspiration by guiding American cuisine into the modern era. That's what a true godfather does for someone or something young and without direction."

Larry's career traces America's culinary roots and reconnects them with modern cuisine. Many of today's chef superstars have built their reputations outside their restaurants. In addition to running acclaimed kitchens, they spread their gospel through Web sites and blogs and, of course, television. When Forgione entered the American culinary scene in the late 1970s, there were no twenty-four-hour television channels devoted to food and cooking. His reputation as a great chef was based on the talent upon which he built a restaurant empire.

A Long Island native, Forgione entered the kitchen without a long-term goal of staying there. As a physical education major at a college in West Virginia, he skipped a semester because he developed pneumonia. When he recovered, a cousin with a catering firm in Brooklyn gave him a job picking through parsley and doing all the things an eighteen-year-old with no experience could do.

But Forgione soon signed on at the posh Breakers Hotel in Palm Beach, Florida. Food appealed to his senses and it was exciting to see the kitchen action. He enrolled in the Culinary Institute of America (CIA), and was in the first graduating class at the Hyde Park campus in 1974. He continues to be an active supporter of the school and is now a member of the admissions committee.

After the CIA, Forgione went to work for Michel Bourdin, formerly of Maxim's in Paris, then heading the restaurants at London's renowned Connaught Hotel. "I was there for more than two years, and each day I would see wonderful new foods we didn't have—the seafood from France, chanterelles and black chanterelles, tiny haricots vert. Why don't we have chanterelles in the United States?" Forgione questioned. "How come they have everything and we seemingly have so little?"

Forgione stayed almost three years in London instead of the one year he'd anticipated. With a newfound appreciation of fine ingredients, he returned to New York in 1977 and worked with chef Michel Guérard at Regine's. Then, Buzzy O'Keefe, the owner of the River Café, lured him in 1979 with the goal of lifting his restaurant to the level of greatness. "I realized it would give me the buying power to develop the products I wanted to use," Forgione recalls. He courted farmers, producers, foragers, fishermen, mycologists, and hunters. It was during this time that he and the legendary James Beard became friends.

Solidifying his principles of cooking, the European experience also stoked Forgione's patriotism. "In the U.S., when someone asks you what you are, you usually say the country where your grandparents were born, but in Europe you say you're an American. In food, I realized my country was getting the short end of the culinary stick." Americans were cooking for convenience, not the natural bounty of locally grown, regional ingredients. Forgione continues to be passionate about his approach, updating and inventing, and treating American foodstuffs with his creative skill.

Beard, who replaced the French masters as Forgione's guru and mentor, validated his approach. "Jim could remember all the foods that have disappeared that he worked to have cultivated again. I looked at the apples on the market, and there are so few, and he would tell me about the ones that used to grow in his yard in Portland," remembers Forgione.

When Forgione was ready to open his own restaurant, Beard remembered a former Manhattan gallery called An American Place that had featured young American artists, including Georgia O'Keeffe. Beard liked the connection between the name and the type of cuisine for which Forgione was building a reputation and suggested it as a name for the new restaurant.

The name "An American Place" reflected both the concept of the dishes and the ingredients comprising them. Forgione wanted to give American food a special integrity by looking to the past and cooking in the present. His food has always reflected this desire, and Forgione doesn't do slavish recreations of historic dishes, even those with distinct roots in the past. He looks at the components of nineteenth-century dishes, for example, and then adds his special touch.

James Beard ate at An American Place every week. Jackie Onassis was a regular. Dan Rather and Warren Beatty claimed their own tables. After restaurateur Danny Meyer, who would later be named the 1996 James Beard Foundation Humanitarian of the Year, sampled the restaurant, he announced that there was a new game in town. Other restaurateurs flocked to see what was going on. "One night, twenty-six of the twenty-eight tables were filled with restaurant critics, food writers, or chefs," the avuncular Forgione remembers.

"Forgione was part of an important and small group of chefs who were at the forefront of the 'new American cuisine movement' in the early 1980s," notes Meyer. "An American Place was the first restaurant in New York that applied the notion of buying seasonal foods from local farmers and using those ingredients to update and improve American classics."

Forgione also showcased American specialties, cooking the kind of American food he envisioned—honest food, nothing contrived; food that tasted and felt good.

"I WANTED THE GREAT INGREDIENTS, AND I BEGAN TO BELIEVE THAT TO GIVE AMERICAN COOKING A PLACE IN THE FUTURE, WE HAVE TO REACH BACK TO THE INTEGRITY OF YESTERDAY," HE SAYS WITH A PROPHET'S CONVICTION.

An American Place changed locations several times before finally closing in 2010. During that time, Forgione earned the title "businessman/chef" by opening restaurants throughout the city. The Grill Room, Marketplace Express, Rosehill, the Coach House, Restaurant Above, and Manhattan Prime all bore the Forgione name. He entered an agreement with the Lord & Taylor department store chain to open a series of Larry Forgione's Signature Cafes around the country, as well. Forgione usually self-financed his expansions,

preferring to maintain control, but he says the motivation for opening new restaurants isn't just financial. Always, the food comes first. He considers himself a "chef-restaurateur," someone who puts restaurants together with the food as the prime consideration.

Forgione has published two cookbooks, *An American Place* and *Heart-Healthy Cooking for All Seasons*. *An American Place* was the recipient of the James Beard Foundation award for Best American Cookbook in 1996.

Most recently, his energies and vast experience are focused on consulting. Forgione consults as the culinary director of Clarke's Group, owners of New York's legendary P. J. Clarke's restaurants, now expanding across the country. He's involved with ingredient sourcing and ensuring a farm-to-table ethos in the restaurant despite its high volume.

He is also the co-founder of American Spoon Foods, a Michigan specialty food company formed in 1981 to produce preserves and jellies using the highest-quality American ingredients. Forgione and Justin Rashid—who foraged for the chef's restaurants—had the idea to make fifty or 100 cases for the restaurants, then make another hundred or so and sell them. The products are available through mail order, as well as at the six stand-alone American Spoon stores and through other outlets.

One event in which Forgione was involved forever changed the dynamics of professional kitchens across the United States. Ten chefs came together in a historic convergence at the American Institute of Wine and Food's first event in San Francisco on May 4, 1983. Held at the Stanford Court Hotel, the new institute's kickoff occasion was launched by the late winemakers Robert Mondavi and Dick Graff, along with Julia Child. It was the first formal gathering of all that talent in one place, cooking together, celebrating American wine and food, showcasing an eight-course dinner for 300 guests.

When Forgione, Jeremiah Tower, Jonathan Waxman, Mark Miller, Paul Prudhomme, Wolfgang Puck, and the other chefs all met, what they had in common was a search for superior ingredients that they could showcase with their simple cooking techniques. "It was just realizing that the freshest is the best," says Forgione. "The other great thing about our generation of chefs is that everybody was very willing to share, very willing to promote the product that they had found, and that they had created."

Those few days of unity, creative stimulation, and hilarity solidified the concepts of engaging the public in an exploration of California wines and American foods. It brought appreciation and focus to what's now known as new American cooking.

Speaking with characteristic reserve, Forgione is nonetheless unwavering, true to his convictions three decades after identifying his direction: "The key to the future of American cooking is to get the ingredients. I remember reading that Fernand Point once said of La Pyramide that you can't have a great food without great ingredients. And I decided that no American-food restaurant could be of world-class caliber until the ingredients were at that level."

The chef is the first to admit that the dishes he creates today could not have been listed on menus when he began, since the raw ingredients were not domestically obtainable. That they are now is due in large part to Forgione's efforts. The influence of his restaurants on American cooking landed him a place as one of LIFE magazine's "50 Most Influential Baby Boomers" in June 1996. No other individual from the restaurant industry was listed.

Now, Forgione's priorities include a deep interest in the development of the craft among younger chefs. "A lot of people don't take the time to build up the strength of their career," observes Forgione. "The successful ones put in the time when they're younger." He is clearly referring to the apprentice tradition and passing on that knowledge as James Beard did for him.

Among youngsters who did put in the time are products of the Forgione household. Three of his four children are in the business. Marc Forgione has his own successful New York restaurant, Restaurant Marc Forgione, and he became an Iron Chef. He did his career the right way in his dad's opinion. "Growing up, Marc worked weekends and holidays at An American Place. He was a little ahead of most graduates from any cooking school because of the experience, so he studied hotel and restaurant management at the University of Massachusetts. Then he went to Michel Guérard's restaurant, now a family tradition, for what was supposed to be a six-month stay. He ended up there for almost a year," says Larry Forgione.

Bryan Forgione followed his father to the CIA, and, like Marc, worked weekends and holidays at An American Place. Bryan owned a barbecue restaurant in Long Beach, New York, and is currently executive chef of Society Café Encore in Las Vegas, Nevada.

Forgione's youngest son, Sean, at first decided to forego the kitchen in favor of a career somewhat similar to being a high-stakes restaurateur—playing Texas Hold'em Poker professionally. But he is now working with his brother, Bryan, in restaurants to gain the knowledge and experience to succeed in the industry. Forgione's daughter, Cara, works in creative services of the marketing and promotions department for a start-up clothing business.

As he did with his children, Forgione has always encouraged budding chefs. Christina Machamer, of Hell's Kitchen and Bouchon Beverly Hills, is among those who have knocked on Forgione's kitchen door and were welcomed. "I decided to start at the top restaurant and work my way down, offering free labor for experience," she says. "I was willing to do anything to get into the best restaurant in St. Louis, which was An American Place. I didn't even have knives."

"He was very paternal and, more than anyone, took an interest in me. Chef took me under his wing," Machamer remembers. After exposing her to the discipline, rigor, and techniques of a professional kitchen, Forgione steered her to the Culinary Institute of America. Following graduation from his alma mater, she competed in Hell's Kitchen, Fox television's ferocious reality-based show. By winning—no small feat of accomplishment—she earned a job with chef Gordon Ramsey. She's now a chef tournant at Thomas Keller's Bouchon in Los Angeles, another step up the culinary training ladder. Other culinary notables that have passed through Forgione's kitchen include Melissa Kelly, Cat Cora, and Michael Cimarusti.

Forgione's generosity in encouraging future chefs is yet another excellent reason to call him "the godfather."

OYSTERS *and* SEA URCHINS SHARING A SHELL

CONCASSÉ

1 teaspoon olive oil

1 teaspoon minced shallots

2 ripe tomatoes, peeled, seeded, and finely diced

2 tablespoons dry white wine

Freshly ground black pepper

SAUCE

3 ounces dry white wine

2 tablespoons white wine vinegar

1 tablespoon sliced shallots

5 or 6 parsley stems

1 teaspoon chopped fresh ginger

Oyster liquor reserved from shucking the oysters

2 tablespoons heavy cream

6 tablespoons unsalted butter, cut into small pieces, at room temperature

2 tablespoons fresh lemon juice

1 tablespoon Worcestershire sauce

2 tablespoons finely sliced fresh chives

Grated zest of ½ lemon

½ teaspoon grated fresh ginger

Sea salt

Freshly ground black pepper

GARNISHES AND OYSTERS

Coarse salt

Fresh seaweed or watercress

Black and pink peppercorns

Julienned fresh ginger

Thyme sprigs

1 dozen fresh oysters, shucked, on the half shell

12 pieces sushi-grade sea urchin roe

Chopped fresh chives

To make the concassé

1. Heat the oil in a sauté pan. When hot, add the shallots and tomatoes and stir. Cook for a minute or two. Add the wine and a few turns of pepper from a mill. Let the mixture simmer for 3 to 4 minutes or until most of the moisture has evaporated. Spoon the concassé into a bowl, set aside, and keep warm.

CONTINUED

To make the sauce

1. Combine the wine, vinegar, shallots, parsley, chopped ginger, and reserved oyster liquor in a small saucepan over medium heat and simmer until reduced to about 2 tablespoons. Add the cream and bring to a rapid simmer to reduce the cream slightly.

2. Lower the heat to very low and whisk in the butter a piece at a time, making sure the pieces of butter are incorporated before adding more butter.

3. When all the butter is incorporated, immediately remove from the heat and add the lemon juice and Worcestershire sauce. Strain through a fine sieve, add the chives, lemon zest, and grated ginger and season with a few turns of pepper from the mill and a pinch of sea salt. Set aside and keep warm.

To serve

1. Preheat the broiler to high. Make a thin bed of coarse salt, seaweed, peppercorns, julienned ginger, and thyme sprigs on each serving plate.

2. Remove the oysters from the shells and set aside in a bowl. Sprinkle coarse salt on a rimmed baking sheet and set the oyster shells on top, making sure they sit stably. Divide the tomato concassé evenly among the shells, then return 1 oyster to each shell. Season each with one turn of a peppermill, and then broil a few inches from the heating element for 2 minutes. Remove from the broiler. Using a fork, turn over each oyster and continue broiling for 1 minute more. Nestle 1 piece of sea urchin roe with the oyster in each shell and continue broiling for 1 minute, or until the sea urchin roe is just warmed through.

3. Set three oysters on the salt bed on each plate. Nap with the sauce and sprinkle with chives. Serve immediately.

SERVES 4

PAN-ROASTED CHICKEN BREAST *with* HERB JUS *and* JIM'S CREAMED HASH POTATOES

JIM'S CREAMED HASH POTATOES

2 large russet potatoes

¼ cup blended olive oil

Salt

Freshly ground black pepper

2 tablespoons finely diced onion

2 tablespoons salted butter

1 teaspoon cornstarch

½ cup heavy cream

1 tablespoon chopped flat-leaf parsley

1 tablespoon chopped chives

CHICKEN

2 tablespoons olive oil

4 boneless skin-on chicken breasts, with first wing bones

Kosher salt

Freshly ground black pepper

HERB JUS

3 garlic cloves, slightly crushed

1 sprig fresh rosemary

1 sprig fresh thyme

2 tablespoons cream sherry

1½ cups dark poultry stock

2 tablespoons unsalted butter

1 tablespoon fresh lemon juice

To make the hash potatoes

1. Bring a large pot of lightly salted water to a rolling boil. Add the potatoes and boil for 30 to 40 minutes until al dente, or slightly firm to the bite. Drain and let cool to room temperature. Remove the skins and cut the potatoes into 3/4-inch dice.

2. In a large nonstick skillet or sauté pan over medium-high heat, warm the oil until shimmering, or just before smoking (365°F). Add the potatoes and sauté until golden. Season with salt and pepper, then drain the potatoes through a sieve to remove the excess oil. Set aside.

3. Preheat the oven to 350°F.

CONTINUED

To cook the chicken

1. In a cast-iron skillet over medium-high heat, warm the oil and swirl to evenly coat the pan. Season the chicken with salt and pepper on both sides.

2. When the oil is hot, pan-fry the chicken breasts, skin-side down for 3 to 4 minutes, or until the skin is brown. With a pair of tongs, move the breasts to loosen them from the pan.

3. Place the pan in the oven for 15 to 18 minutes, or until the chicken is just cooked through.

4. Remove the chicken breasts and let them rest on a cooling rack in a warm place.

To make the jus

1. Pour off the oil from chicken pan and add the garlic, rosemary, and thyme. Put the pan over medium-high heat. Add the sherry and stir to scrape up the browned bits from the bottom of the pan. Add the stock. Reduce to ¼ cup and remove from the heat. Whisk in the butter, lemon juice, and any drippings from the chickens as they rest. Drain the jus through a fine sieve and keep warm.

To finish the hash potatoes

1. Return the potatoes to the nonstick skillet over medium-high heat, and add the onion and butter. Continue to cook, stirring, for another 2 to 3 minutes.

2. Dissolve the cornstarch in the cream and add it to the potatoes. Bring them to a boil and simmer for another 2 to 3 minutes. Stir in the parsley and chives.

3. Spoon creamed hash browns in the center of each plate. Place a chicken breast on top. Pour the jus around the hash browns and serve immediately.

SERVES 4

1993

A TRIBUTE TO

JEAN-LOUIS PALLADIN

CHAPTER *four*

Only one of our James Beard Outstanding Chef Award winners is no longer with us. Jean-Louis Palladin died of lung cancer in 2001 at the age of fifty-five. Jean-Louis arrived in Washington, D.C., in 1979 from Gascony, France, and was the youngest chef ever to receive two Michelin stars.

He opened Jean-Louis at the Watergate, which became an immediate destination for serious food lovers all over the country. Palladin was also a magnet for French chefs looking to make the move to America to find freedom to cook creatively and realize their potential. Daniel Boulud and Eric Ripert, both Outstanding Chef Award winners, attribute their success, in part, to the advice and support they received from Palladin.

No one ever really quite knew what to expect when they were with Jean-Louis Palladin, except that there would be another splendid adventure. Palladin's unmistakable look made him a celebrity in a city filled with political stars. Oversized glasses sat above a thick moustache on a ruddy face topped with curly brown hair.

Gleeful mischief and open-handed generosity characterized Palladin. He wrapped his wings around the young French chefs arriving in the United States. He led them on an exuberant ride, often on motorcycles, as they cooked, caroused, and learned the ins and outs of survival in a new country.

"He was definitely a chef's chef," says Michel Richard. "Everybody has a story about how Jean-Louis called them up and said, 'You gotta buy from this cheesemaker or they'll go out of business.' There's a tremendous amount of continuous impact that he has had, whether it's through the farmers or through the culture of today's chefs—he was very much what made a lot of it happen. I see young chefs today and I think the successes are because of Jean-Louis's influence."

In fact, Richard came to Washington, D.C., because Palladin made it an interesting place. Eric Ripert learned to rock when Palladin was rolling. A lonely Jean-Georges Vongerichten was introduced around by Palladin. The late Gilbert Le Coze came to visit. Ariane Daguin, a Gascony native, arrived in Washington as a young woman, then founded D'Artagnan, a purveyor of gourmet products, game, poultry, and foie gras. Palladin made her welcome as a fellow countryman should, including her in the social whirl.

He organized game hunts, foraging expeditions, motorcycle road trips, hang gliding exploits, and skydiving picnics to blow off steam with other chefs. He famously parachuted while his former wife screamed, "Don't do that, don't do that!" He made it a point to pull local chefs together into a tight restaurant community, encouraging people who were struggling for recognition.

"To work in Palladin's kitchen meant that you were at times the object of his passion and intensity," remembers Jimmy Sneed, who worked for Palladin before opening his own restaurant, The Frog and the Redneck, in nearby Virginia. Sneed walked into Palladin's kitchen looking for a job. Asked only if he spoke French, he answered "Oui, Chef," and was working within minutes.

The chef was not above raising his voice in the heat of preparing a service. But Sneed says Palladin's yelling wasn't malicious. "It wasn't from anger or meant to be demeaning. He yelled because what he was about to put on that plate was the most important thing in his world." Palladin believed every bite was used to judge him.

Maîtres Cuisiniers
de France

Vous a préparé spécialement pour cette soirée :

La Soupe d'échalotes aux émincés de chevreuil et
aux petits choux verts aux œufs de Cailles .
....
La Terrine de nouilles fraîches au foie gras de canard
et aux truffes, coulis de tomates au basilic.
....
La Cassolette d'écrevisses aux champignons sauvages .
....
Le Râble de Lapereau, son foie et ses rognons.
farci et braisé aux carottes nouvelles.
La Mousseline de céleris raves.
....
L'Oiseau surprise à l'armagnac.
....
Les Raviolis de pêches confites à la crème d'abricots
au gingembre.
Les Sorbets mandarine, noix de coco et fruit de la Passion.
au coulis de framboises .
Les Petits fours
....
Washington DC, le 15 Avril 1984

Académie culinaire
de France

"The yelling and screaming came from the passion and intensity—the importance of getting it right at that moment," according to Sneed.

Palladin was unrelenting, believing that cooking required a dedication to be placed above everything else. His work ethic was legendary. He was not a television chef or one who split his time between his restaurant and other business ventures. For most of Palladin's career in Washington, D.C., he rarely left the city. When he was in Washington, he could be found in his restaurant's kitchen six nights a week. "You need to say to your wife, if you have a wife, 'I'm sorry, but you will need to be second in my life,'" he said in 1997. "Being in the restaurant ten, twelve, fourteen hours a day—that's your family.'"

"He wanted everyone to appreciate using the freshest and the best items in their kitchens," says Richard. "And he wanted to ensure that the people who provided those ingredients survived and flourished.

"Jean-Louis once went up to Maine to search for wonderful fish," remembers Sneed. "Rod Mitchell is a seafood purveyor now, but back then he was just a local fisherman. But that's where scallops were shelled. You got divers to go down to the ocean floor and get scallops and Rod went into business doing that."

John and Sukey Jamison personally delivered three lambs when Palladin wanted to sample them from their Jamison Farms in Latrobe, Pennsylvania. John remembers the first time they met: "In my high school French, I told the maître d' that we had *trois agneau* for the chef. With a nod, a cook ran in to take the lambs. 'Ah *oui*, Chef has been waiting for you; please come in.' Sukey and I stayed back partly to be out of the line of fire should there be a problem. All I could see was the tall chef with the S.O.S. hair wildly waving his arms. I said to Sukey, 'This is either very good or very bad.' He motioned us to join him. His eyes were moist. Jean-Louis said, 'I am so happy to meet you. You have to excuse me because these lambs are so beautiful. They remind me of the ones I bought when I was an apprentice. These are a souvenir of my youth.'" The Jamisons became his friends, as well as longtime purveyors.

Palladin's devotion to quality ingredients was the result of his memories of eating in his native Gascony, where farmers and hunters provided food for his family's meals. Condom, Palladin's home town, is a tiny village in the Pyrenees next to Basque country. It is famous for foie gras, Armagnac, and abundant sunflower and lavender fields. But Palladin considered himself an American chef with a French mind.

When he was inducted into the tight-knit society of Maîtres Cuisinier de France, he celebrated accordingly. Inductees traditionally provide a feast for members and friends. In Palladin's instance, there were eighty guests. He smuggled 400 illegal ortolans into the United States for the occasion (hidden from customs in a box of his daughter's diapers).

"It's not illegal to hunt them for personal use, but they are forbidden to be sold," explains Daguin. "Normally, a table of six close friends might enjoy the delicacy. To serve to eighty is astonishing."

The traditional way to eat ortolans is to consume almost the entire bird with your head covered by a cloth. The headgear allows the diner to inhale all the roasted bird's earthy, rich aroma. Palladin sneered at the idea that the covering of the diners' heads was to hide their shame. "Shame? Mais non!" Palladin said in Stewart Lee Allen's book, *The Devil's Garden: A Sinful History of Forbidden Food*. Instead, he offered that it is done out of deference or reverence, as if bowing one's head in prayer.

At a young age, Palladin's parents began training his palate to appreciate the fresh foods that would become the hallmark of his cooking. Sneed, who continued to be a close friend, says that Jean-Louis's early years were a driving influence. "He had such an intensity and such a memory. He could remember a dish that he ate or cooked twenty years before."

Palladin's mother worked as a nurse during the week and cooked in a local restaurant on Sundays. Owner René Sandrini eventually offered Jean-Louis a job as well. Sandrini become not only a mentor, but also a treasured friend.

After attending hotel school and apprenticing in Paris and Monte Carlo, Palladin and Sandrini renovated a fourteenth-century monastery, opening La Table des Cordeliers there in 1968. The restaurant, named after an order of monks, served more than three hundred dinners on the weekend, which was amazing in a small town.

Palladin earned two Michelin stars by the age of twenty-eight, becoming the youngest chef in France to achieve that honor. Seeking a name-brand chef, owners of the Watergate Hotel lured him to Washington, D.C., in 1979, using the restaurant to attract well-heeled clientele into purchasing apartments in the complex. Palladin created dishes at the forty-two-seat restaurant that changed the face of dining in the nation's capital. His insistence on using the freshest ingredients, no matter the cost in obtaining them, meant that throughout the restaurant's life, profit was not the driving force behind the establishment.

Shortly after Palladin arrived at the Watergate, a retired state department officer came to him with air-puffed plastic bags of misted, hand-raised baby herbs. According to the restaurant's sous-chef, Palladin cast his eyes heavenward and said, "I believe that God sent you to me." That contributor, too, became a purveyor for many years.

Palladin published one book of his recipes, *Jean-Louis: Cooking with the Seasons*. The recipes within were grouped into menus and divided by season. With lush photography by the acclaimed late Fred J. Maroon, it is an oversized art book and a celebration of the foods and ingredients that Palladin found in America.

When Palladin was diagnosed with lung cancer in his early fifties, colleagues and friends held a series of fundraisers to help with his mounting medical bills. It was a tribute to a man who had given so much to the profession that he loved.

"If we don't celebrate our heroes, nobody will," commented Charlie Trotter at Palladin's memorial service in 2001. Two hundred people gathered at the Omni Shoreham Hotel in Washington, D.C., to honor the friend and mentor who, in this country, paired French technique and contemporary flair with the best and freshest American ingredients. Guests included renowned chefs from all over the country—and a handful from France, in addition to loyal patrons of the restaurant and purveyors. Many California chefs took the red-eye to Washington just to pay their respects.

"When I was a young cook, I saved money to come here from New York, eat by myself, and stay at the Howard Johnson Hotel across the street," says Thomas Keller of The French Laundry in California's Napa Valley.

"HE LIVED WHAT YOU NEED TO HAVE TO BE A CHEF—THE WORK ETHIC, THE PASSION, THE FOCUS. HE SET SO MANY STANDARDS FOR ME.

To have him first as a role model, then a colleague, and then a friend has got to be one of the greatest things that has happened to me in my life," remembers Keller.

"His was the first kitchen in America I stepped into," says Daniel Boulud, who was the chef at the European Commission in Washington, D.C., in the early 1980s. "I had worked with people he admired in France, but here I was a private chef. When I decided to go to New York, he said, 'If you need anything, let me know.' He always supported me—when he heard the Westbury Hotel was looking for a chef for the Polo Lounge in late 1982, and later when I interviewed to go to Le Cirque, he was always behind me."

After his death, the Jean-Louis Palladin Foundation was created by his friends and colleagues to carry on his legacy. The foundation established a grant so that working chefs could learn more about his passion: sourcing and cooking with the finest and freshest ingredients available. Since 2009, the James Beard Foundation has administered the Jean-Louis Palladin Professional Work/Study Initiative.

1994

DANIEL BOULUD

CHAPTER *five*

A SIDE TABLE IN DANIEL BOULUD'S OFFICE DISPLAYS PHOTOGRAPHS AND MEMORABILIA: SHAQUILLE O'NEAL'S AUTOGRAPHED SHOE, FOR EXAMPLE. It's a U.S. size 23—16¹/2 inches by 6 inches. Hard to believe it fits a man's foot. The space is organized as a study with comfortable banquettes, a dining area for four people, and a television. The chef's office is called "the skybox," since its two large windows overlook the kitchen arena below and the kitchen staff can look up. Many of the international crew are World Cup Soccer and Tour de France enthusiasts, so the television is especially important for team spirit at game time.

The morning after the James Beard Foundation honored Daniel as Outstanding Restaurant 2010, Boulud hung the coveted medallion from a rack in the kitchen that holds an array of silver cloches, so the crew could share the glory. "We work very much as a team," he says. As Manhattan's preeminent chef, Boulud's shoes are as hard to fill as O'Neal's giant sneakers, yet he nurtures his staff. In crisp double-breasted whites, de rigueur for the affable, well-groomed gentleman-chef, Boulud is remarkably relaxed and at ease in pristine surroundings, which contribute to assuring his guests and employees that they're experiencing the apex of culinary arts.

The restaurant Daniel on Manhattan's Upper East Side opened in 1993. The Dinex Group LLC was created in 1997 by Boulud and partners Joel Smilow and Lili Lynton, approximately four years after Daniel was opened. Together for almost two decades, they have a dozen establishments. Epicerie Boulud and Boulud Sud opened in the spring of 2011, offering different dining styles and price points. With other restaurants in Palm Beach, London, Singapore, Beijing, and most recently, Miami, the company takes a very hands-on approach and trains its teams to operate á la Boulud. Boulud is clearly the driving force, but he credits his cadre of operations directors, corporate chefs, wine director, financial department, human resources, and communications staff with overseeing each restaurant and keeping very tight quality, service, training, and cost control.

In 2009, Boulud spent a substantial sum renovating Daniel. "What am I going to do? Own a château in France? So I put it back here," he says of his profits. To keep his staff happy and motivated, he continues to invest in his restaurants. As for himself, Boulud is like the chairman of the board. "I'm everything. I'm the one who manages nothing and yet sees everything because everyone on my team has responsibilities to manage. They are all a part of this success, and then from one restaurant, two restaurants, three restaurants . . . "

Boulud is always looking for new food inspirations and talent. "We keep evolving. I travel a lot. I'm opening up a restaurant in Singapore and we have a restaurant in Beijing. We have a restaurant in London. And all this is a product of having established a reputation for consistent quality and caring, and working with partners who want to bring my very particular style of French-American cooking to their locations. It's a progression of new ideas reinterpreted for new places and a desire to grow as a team."

Boulud now envisions a trend of more casual, medium-priced restaurants that offer value to the customer. That is the focus of DBGB Kitchen and Bar, the restaurant he opened on the Bowery in New York in 2010. It's also the case for db Bistro Moderne, which Boulud has found to be a model that translates well to other cities. "A lot of young chefs in America are taking that route," he says. "Many of them learn in these fancy places but are opening up very casual places, and they're very good cooks. I think it's really good. It really shows that the culinary foundation in this country is very solid now. And a young cook can show that he or she can become a very, very good chef."

Although Boulud stands at the pinnacle of the industry with numerous restaurants, awards, and world-class cuisine in elegant surroundings, he still has a taste for food and people that are a little less grand. He seldom cooks at home, but when he does, he cooks a wide range of cusines. "I love Chinese cooking because it's so quick. The vegetables are fresh and it's so good. French cuisine isn't always the perfect solution in every situation," he admits. Boulud takes great pleasure in cooking with his daughter Alix, recently graduated from Tufts University, outside of Boston.

He also pays homage to the home cook: "Sometimes the best food I've eaten is from a home cook. They don't depend on recipe books because they cook instinctively. They went to the market, bought some stuff, and they are cooking. And that's what cooking is about, first and foremost. That's why I'm always asking my cooks to make me something, to make me a salad, make me an omelet, and make me the best of anything that you think you can make without fancy ingredients. I don't need caviar. I don't need truffles . . . Make me something creative, well executed."

"I got here through street smarts," Boulud acknowledges, although he is as sophisticated and urbane as an uptown banker. "I learned the hard way. I started at fourteen as an apprentice and kept going until I was seventeen and a half. I opted out of culinary school early on—it was too academic and not hands-on enough for me. Studying wasn't my thing at the time. I wanted real experience, right in the kitchen. But I wish I had done it differently—had the education first and then the apprenticeship." He explains, "In today's competitive world, I think it's important to get a good education first and then nurture your talent."

After being a finalist for best cooking apprentice in France, Boulud went on to train under such renowned chefs as Roger Vergé, Georges Blanc, and Michel Guérard. Following two years in Copenhagen, where Boulud worked as a chef at the Plaza Hotel, he moved to Washington, D.C., to work as a private chef for the European Commission.

French restaurants in America in the early 1980s were old-fashioned, Boulud believes. "That all changed with the late Jean-Louis Palladin. He was the one who pushed to bring French cuisine in America up to date because it was very monochromatic in the sense that every restaurant was doing the same thing. With a few exceptions, there wasn't much personality or creativity."

It was Palladin who later introduced him to the group that owned the Polo Lounge at the Westbury Hotel in Manhattan, where he moved to be the opening chef. He next went to Le Régence at the Hotel Plaza Athenée in New York, and then finally he was named executive chef at Le Cirque—a restaurant regularly chosen as one of the best in the country during his tenure from 1987 to 1993.

When Boulud was at the Polo Lounge as executive sous-chef, he remembers a "talented and organized" young chef de partie there who admired what chefs were doing in France and was determined to be their equal. He was Thomas Keller, who also went on to become a James Beard Foundation Outstanding Chef in 1997. Boulud remembers, "Thomas was just a good chef. And in the team, not everyone is equal. But when you have somebody who is super good, you really notice. And he was the super good one. He wanted just to learn. The funny thing is that Elizabeth Marie Keller, Thomas's mother, was working in the restaurant business as well. Thomas grew up helping out in the restaurant where his mother worked which, ironically, is the current location of Café Boulud in Palm Beach."

The fraternity of chefs has strong connections, with each generation leading the next. Alumni from Daniel Boulud's kitchens who have gone on to succeed on their own also include Jonathan Benno, who was executive chef at Thomas Keller's Per Se and is now the chef of Lincoln at Lincoln Center; Bill Telepan, chef-owner of Telepan; Michael Anthony at Gramercy Tavern; and David Chang of Momofuku. The list reads like a who's who of extraordinary chefs.

The inspiration for Boulud's cuisine is rooted in his native France, which he combines with a contemporary, creative spin. "I would say that the hardware is French, but the software can be more local and more spontaneous and certainly a combination of flavors. Even if I use Asian ingredients, I always think French balance and seasoning. So what is French balance and seasoning? Nothing too spicy, too smoky, or too strong," he declares. Other inspirations come from where he happens to be at a particular time. "I've always been inspired by where I am, the season, and what's in the local market."

Boulud's cooking is technically complicated but the execution looks simple. "We have fun cooking, and I don't want people to suffer through a painfully long night just so we can show them a sixteen-course meal. Rather, all the dishes, each set of courses, is right on the money. They're focused."

In addition to simply staying ahead in the international restaurant world, Boulud has kept his competitive edge by continuously upgrading and improving his restaurants. Every afternoon at Daniel, for example, there's a class on some aspect of service. The wait staff takes part in a training session, followed by an exam. "We want them to have an opportunity to grow. It's a good thing because it really motivates us to be better both from the employee and management perspective. Good service is service you're barely aware of. And so we work very hard on that. And we apply the same standards to each of our restaurants, whether they are bistros or fine dining," he notes. "We want our group to know what's going on in the industry and in food media. We make them read the *New York Times* every Wednesday. Everybody has to read the food critics' point of view to understand what's important to our diners."

Boulud believes that service must be totally professional and unobtrusive, allowing the food to be the star, with a sense of caring for the comfort of people. "Because this all could be very pompous and intimidating," he acknowledges. "My standard for service comes from Paris, where there is such precision but also warmth and friendliness in even the greatest restaurants. And it's not every restaurant that can accomplish that. At Daniel we have a lot of regulars and, of course, the regulars attract our attention because we have a relationship with them. So they want to talk, they want to chat, they know the names of the waiters and busboys; they know who just had a baby, so they bring a gift. I mean, it's more than the food—it's a family. But the staff also knows new potential regulars walk in every day. After 9/11, I felt like I needed to worry not only about every one of my staff but about every one of my customers. And so we made some big changes in order to work harder at offering better service, taking care of people."

Boulud's gift is not only his talent as a chef but his active interest in his staff and his guests. As much as outstanding food is his focus, so are the people around him who, he would probably say, have helped make him a success.

MAINE PEEKYTOE CRAB SALAD *with* CELERY, WALNUT OIL, AND GRANNY SMITH APPLE

APPLE PICKLE COINS

2 Granny Smith apples, peeled, sliced 1/2-inch thick, and cut into 1-inch-diameter rounds

1 cup rice vinegar

2 1/2 tablespoons sugar

APPLE CIDER GELÉE

1 1/2 sheets gelatin

Ice water

1 cup apple cider

1 1/2 teaspoons poppy seeds

GRANNY SMITH APPLE CONFIT

2 Granny Smith apples, julienned into twelve 2-by-1/2-inch batons

1/2 cup walnut oil

1 teaspoon celery salt

CELERY ROOT PURÉE

1/2 large celery root, cut in 1-inch dice

1 cup milk

Salt

Ground white pepper

CRAB SALAD

1 1/2 tablespoons celery root brunoise

8 ounces Maine Peekytoe crabmeat, picked over

2 tablespoons Granny Smith apple brunoise

1 1/2 tablespoons mayonnaise

1 teaspoon New Orleans Creole mustard

1 teaspoon chopped fresh chives

1/2 teaspoon cider vinegar

1/2 teaspoon walnut oil

Salt

Ground white pepper

3 Granny Smith apples, cut into twelve 8-by-3-inch sheets with Chiba Peels Turning Slicer

1 lemon, juiced

1/4 cup crushed walnuts

APPLE SKIN CHIPS

1 Macintosh apple

Canola oil, for frying

To make the apple pickle coins

1. Put the rounds into a shallow heatproof container. In a small saucepan over medium heat, bring the vinegar and sugar to a simmer. Pour over the apples. Cover and refrigerate overnight or up to 3 days. Strain before plating.

To make the apple cider gelée

1. Soak the gelatin sheets in a bowl of ice water for 20 minutes. Squeeze dry.

CONTINUED

2. In a medium saucepan over medium heat, warm the cider to just below a simmer. Add the poppy seeds and gelatin, stirring to dissolve the gelatin. Pour into an uncovered 6-inch square dish. Refrigerate. When set, slice the gelée into twelve ½-by-½-inch cubes. Reserve, chilled.

To make the apple confit
1. In a small saucepan over medium heat, combine the apples, oil, and salt and bring to just below a simmer. Cover and cook, stirring occasionally, until the apples are tender, about 15 minutes. Refrigerate.

To make the celery root purée
1. In a medium saucepan over medium heat, combine the celery root and milk. Add enough water to cover. Season with salt and pepper and bring to a simmer. Cook until tender. In a blender or food processor, purée the celery root with enough of the cooking liquid to make a smooth, thick purée. Refrigerate and adjust the seasonings before plating.

To make the crab salad
1. In a small pot, bring water to a boil. Add the celery root brunoise and cook until tender, about 1 minute. Drain and let cool.

2. In a medium bowl, combine the crabmeat, apple, celery root, mayonnaise, mustard, chives, vinegar, and walnut oil. Season with salt and pepper.

3. Place the apple sheets on a flat surface and brush them lightly with the lemon juice. Divide the crab salad evenly among the 12 sheets, mounding it on the ends closest to you. Tightly roll the sheet away from you to encase the crab salad. Coat the exposed crab at the open ends with some of the crushed walnuts. Repeat with the remaining ingredients. Refrigerate and reserve for no more than 1 hour.

To make the apple chips
1. Using a sharp peeler, remove thin 1-inch-wide strips of apple skin. Use the back of a paring knife to scrape away any excess flesh. Fill a medium saucepan one-third full with oil and bring it to 275°F on a deep-fat thermometer. Put the skins into the saucepan and fry until crisp, about 4 minutes. Transfer to a paper towel–lined plate to drain. Reserve in a dry container at room temperature.

2. To plate, place three rolls of crab salad on each chilled salad plate. Garnish each plate with dots of celery root purée, three pieces of apple cider gelée, three pieces of apple confit, and a few apple pickle coins.

SERVES 4

ROASTED LAMB LOIN *with* TREVISO MARMALADE, SEARED FENNEL, POLENTA TUILES, *and* SICILIAN OLIVE TAPENADE

TREVISO MARMALADE

3 heads Treviso radicchio

Ice water

2 tablespoons olive oil

1 small Spanish onion, cut into brunoise

⅓ cup brunoise of red beets (about 2 ounces)

2 tablespoons red wine vinegar

Salt

Ground white pepper

1 tablespoon balsamic vinegar

OLIVE AND LEMON TAPENADE

¼ cup diced Sicilian olives

¼ cup diced salt-cured Meyer lemon skin

1 teaspoon cracked black pepper

Olive oil

POLENTA

3½ cups chicken stock

1 cup polenta

¾ cup heavy cream

2 large eggs

1 large egg yolk

Fennel pollen

POLENTA TUILES

17½ ounces reserved cooked polenta

1 large egg yolk

1½ teaspoons mascarpone cheese

Pinch fennel pollen

SEARED FENNEL

3 fennel bulbs, halved

2 sprigs fresh thyme

2 tablespoons lemon oil

Pinch espelette pepper (see Note)

Pinch fennel pollen

Ice water

Olive oil

FENNEL PURÉE

1 pound spinach leaves

Ice water

1 tablespoon olive oil, plus extra for purée

1 fennel bulb, sliced thin

Reserved fennel scraps from sous vide fennel

¼ cup chicken stock

½ cup plus 2 tablespoons heavy cream

½ bunch fresh dill, leaves picked

LAMB LOIN

2 lamb loins (about 1 pound each), trimmed

Olive oil

2 garlic cloves, crushed

2 sprigs fresh thyme

2 tablespoons butter

Reserved Treviso radicchio leaves from Treviso Marmalade

Oregano oil

Baby fennel, shaved

Lamb jus infused with oregano

CONTINUED

To make the Treviso marmalade

1. Separate the Treviso leaves and reserve the 2-inch tips of 12 nice leaves in ice water for garnish. Rinse the remaining leaves well, dry, and chop finely. Heat the oil in a large casserole over medium-high heat. Add the onion and sauté until golden brown. Add the beets and sauté until tender. Add the Treviso and red wine vinegar and season with salt and pepper. Simmer until the moisture has almost evaporated, about 20 minutes. Add the balsamic vinegar and simmer to a glazed consistency. Adjust the seasoning. Keep warm.

To make the olive and lemon tapenade

1. In a small bowl, combine the olives, lemon skin, and pepper. Add a drizzle of olive oil and toss to loosely coat. Chill and reserve.

To make the polenta

1. Preheat the oven to 225°F. In a large saucepan, bring the stock to a boil. Stirring constantly, steadily add the polenta. Reduce the heat and simmer, stirring occasionally, until all the stock is absorbed. Season with salt. Weigh out $17\frac{1}{2}$ ounces of the cooked polenta for the tuiles and reserve. In a blender, combine the cream, eggs, yolk, and season with fennel pollen, salt, and pepper. Add the remaining polenta and purée until well combined. Adjust the seasoning.

2. Line a 9-inch square baking pan with buttered parchment paper. Add the polenta purée and bake until set, approximately 1 1/2 hours. Refrigerate. When cold, cut into 1-by-$\frac{1}{2}$-inch logs.

To make the polenta tuiles

1. Preheat the oven to 325°F. In a small bowl, combine the reserved polenta, yolk, mascarpone, and fennel pollen. Season with salt and pepper. Line a baking sheet with a silicone baking mat. Using a 3-by-1-inch template and an offset spatula, spread the mixture onto the template to make thin rectangles. Repeat until the baking sheet is full. Bake for 12 minutes. Let cool.

To make the seared fennel

1. Sous vide the fennel, thyme, lemon oil, and espelette pepper and pollen by cooking in a water bath with an immersion circulator set at 194°F. Cook until the fennel is tender, $1\frac{1}{2}$ to 2 hours. (Alternative method: Combine the fennel, thyme, lemon oil, espelette, and fennel pollen in a nonreactive saucepan. Cover with water and bring to boil. Simmer uncovered until the fennel is tender when pierced, 15 to 20 minutes.)

2. Chill in ice water. Slice the fennel into 12 wedges. Reserve the scraps. When ready to serve, season the wedges with salt, pepper, and pollen. In a medium sauté pan, warm olive oil and sear the slices until browned on both sides.

To make the fennel purée

1. Bring a medium pot of salted water to a boil. Boil the spinach leaves until tender, plunging them immediately into ice water. Squeeze dry and reserve the bowl of ice water.

2. In a 12-inch sauté pan over medium heat, warm the oil. Add the sliced fennel, season with salt and pepper, and stir until tender. Add the fennel scraps and toss to combine. Add the stock and cream. Simmer on low heat until reduced to by half.

3. Transfer the fennel to a blender. Add the spinach and dill. Blend to make a smooth, thick purée. Stream in a few tablespoons of olive oil to emulsify. Using a spatula, press the purée through a fine sieve over a medium bowl. Place the bowl of purée over the bowl of ice water to chill quickly. Once cold, transfer it to a squeeze bottle. Reheat when ready to serve.

To make the lamb

1. Bring the lamb to room temperature and season on all sides with salt and pepper. In a 12-inch sauté pan, heat a thin layer of oil over medium-high heat. Add the lamb and sear on all sides until browned. Reduce the heat to medium; add the garlic, thyme, and butter, basting until medium-rare (about 140°F on a meat thermometer). Remove from the pan and let rest for 8 minutes. Portion the lamb into 6 servings.

To serve

1. Heat six dinner plates. For each serving, place 2 spoonfuls of Treviso marmalade on one side of the plate and arrange a serving of lamb loin on top. Top the lamb loin with a spoonful of olive tapenade and garnish with two leaves of fresh Treviso. Place two polenta tuiles on each side of the loin. Squeeze five dots of fennel purée in a line through the center of the plate. Squeeze small drops of oregano oil in the center of the fennel purée. On the other side of the plate, line three polenta logs in a line. Place two pieces of seared fennel between the polenta. Garnish the top with shaved fennel. At the table, pour over lamb jus infused with oregano.

NOTE: Espelette pepper is a pepper from the small Basque town of Espelette on the border between France and Spain. It is a staple of Basque cuisine. Because it only rates a 4000 on the Scoville scale, it is classified as "not hot."

SERVES 6

1995

RICK BAYLESS

CHAPTER *six*

AS A BOY OF FOURTEEN VACATIONING IN MEXICO WITH HIS FAMILY IN THE 1970S, RICK BAYLESS WAS CAPTIVATED WITH THE EVERYDAY STREET FOOD. "THE FIRST THING THAT WON MY HEART WAS THE VITALITY AND LIFE AND THE PULSE," HE REMEMBERS. "People walking around the park, vendors selling street foods, roaming bands playing music, and bundles of balloons. The second thing that captured me was going into a fabulously old restaurant. I'm a kid used to Tex-Mex food. There was none of it on the menu—not one thing I recognized." But a plate of enchiladas, covered with a brown sauce, made an indelible impression on the young Bayless. "I'll never forget that first taste. That one bite. Mole poblano. I thought, 'This is the food of the gods.'"

The experience was the beginning of Bayless's lifelong love affair with Mexico and its food, resulting in his emergence as America's foremost cook and ambassador of that country's authentic regional cuisine. He's built a culinary mountain on mole, a multi-ingredient sauce of such complexity and diversity that it's taken him from Mexico's home kitchens to the White House.

Bayless was raised in Oklahoma. The state's proximity to the border made Mexico a quick escape whenever he had time during his Spanish and Latin American studies in college. In 1978, he auditioned and won a spot to host a public television program about Mexican cooking, and was sent on two trips to Mexico for research. As he learned more and more about Mexican cooking, he also took to television—he was a natural, prepped by regular appearances on his mother's local morning TV show and by participation in theater groups as a youngster.

Bayless's feel for Mexican food evolved, along with his appreciation for the country, its customs, and its people. "I like earthy cultures and gutsiness. The vitality in Mexico is like nowhere else," he enthuses. But most of all, he remained fascinated by the unheralded street food, the bold, spirited fare he could most often afford.

In 1981, Bayless and his wife Deann were immersed in a study of Mexico's cuisine and culture. When they met, he was aiming for a doctorate in linguistics following undergraduate and graduate work in Spanish and Latin American studies. She was on a similar academic path, acquiring masters' degrees in English and theater, and writing computer manuals. They packed everything into storage and began crisscrossing Mexico by highway and rail. Grabbing and paying for tacos through the window of a slowing but never-stopping train was fast food. The conditions of the roads and buses—and sometimes the driver—were dangerous, and Bayless credits their safe journeys to saints perched on rearview mirrors watching over them.

The Baylesses observed and documented traditional Mexican cooks with the thoroughness of anthropologists. Bayless was amazed at how passionate Mexicans were about their food. The couple planned to stay a year, but overall spent almost eight years there, doing occasional consulting for a small chain of Mexican restaurants in Los Angeles to feed their travel habit.

Bayless remembers, "We spent time in the different marketplaces throughout Mexico. We were welcomed, and even the shy cooks shared their recipes. It was surprising to discover that what was being cooked in homes in Mexico was quite different from what was cooked in America and called Mexican food." Without being intrusive, Bayless perfected a technique for gaining insight into the Mexican food culture. He never asked for recipes. He asked questions. Ultimately, the cooks and vendors would be engaged in conversations that revealed what he needed to know. If he needed more specifics, he'd return. But he never wrote anything in front of them, committing the conversations to memory and later writing down the content.

The Bayless's exploration of the relationships between Mexico and its indigenous foods became the groundwork for a restaurant they dreamed of opening in the United States. At the same time, they went from scholarship to authorship with the publication of their first book, *Authentic Mexican: Regional Cooking from the Heart of Mexico*. That was when Bayless called his doctoral advisor and explained that the dissertation had evolved into a book, and the Ph.D. went by the wayside.

That first book was published the same day in 1987 that the couple opened Frontera Grill in Chicago. From the beginning, the response to both was overwhelmingly favorable. Bayless was in the kitchen the day the restaurant opened and still is today. Deann continues to control the front of the house operations.

In Chicago, Bayless presents the authentic flavors of Mexico and amplifies that cuisine's image in his trio of restaurants. Sharing an entrance to the contemporary Frontera Grill is Topolobampo, one of the few Mexican fine-dining establishments in America. Next door, on the casual side is Xoco, featuring great street food. He's also opened some Frontera Fresco quick-serve operations in the Macy's department store in San Francisco and Chicago, and a restaurant called Red O in Los Angeles.

The couple became experts in Mexican regional folk-art traditions and they continue to build an art collection as a signature of their restaurants. The exuberance of bold, colorful artwork mirrors the excitement from the kitchen to the dining rooms.

Bayless has almost singlehandedly changed how America views and cooks Mexican food. He balances a packed schedule as chef, restaurateur, author, media personality, philanthropist, consultant, and public speaker. A superb communicator, he taps into modern technology's social networks, maintaining an active Twitter feed about cooking and his travels—and it really is Bayless doing the tweeting. An example: "I am the luckiest man in the world. At the stunning Posada Tepozteco cooking dinner with amazingly talented chefs!" (5:17 PM Jul 6). His twittering is yet another avenue to teach people about food. His greatest outreach, though, is through his public television series, *Mexico—One Plate at a Time*, now in its seventh season.

Bayless is also a pioneer in the restaurant business who has taken environmental initiatives ranging from biodegradable takeout packaging, to composting food waste, to buying locally produced foods from Midwestern farmers.

Helping family farms stay afloat is Bayless's rallying cause. He decided to connect with local farms for a better variety of products long ago. "It just makes my life more interesting," he says. "As a chef, I wasn't really interested as much in organics as I was in local and seasonal, but the more I worked with local farmers, the more they taught me about sustainability and what it meant to grow something organically." The Bayless family and restaurant staff created the Frontera Farmer Foundation, seeking to protect Midwestern farmland from development and help small farmers stay competitive with large factory farms. These small producers are a lifeline for the kind of unusual ingredients and quality that Bayless prizes. When Bayless won *Top Chef Masters 2009*, where world-renowned chefs competed for $100,000 to be given to the charity of choice, his prize went to the Frontera Farmer Foundation. More than $500,000 has been granted to farmers since 2003.

Bayless is also a huge proponent of urban agriculture. He took a particularly unique step on the flat roof of his complex of restaurants. Despite the cold Chicago winters, tomatoes, chiles, and other ingredients are grown there and sent straight down to the kitchen. "Rooftop salsa" appears on the menu. "I was always thinking that we have this flat roof above the restaurants we could use for something beneficial," he notes.

Resourceful, observant, and mindful of the environment, Bayless took an idea and expanded it. Not only does the garden provide the restaurant with fresh ingredients, but it also makes a statement about energy conservation and recycling. The green roof is a natural insulator and kitchen scraps become compost for the garden. Behind the Bayless home, greens, edible flowers, and herbs also are grown in a 1,000-square-foot plot for the restaurants. Even basement space is used: They grow microgreens under fluorescent lights for winter salads.

Bayless's culinary background is also home grown. The Oklahoma City native is the fourth generation of a family of restaurateurs and grocers specializing in local barbecue. His parents gave him a copy of Julia Child's *Mastering the Art of French Cooking* when other kids were receiving GI Joe gear. Julia Child fascinated him. He knew exactly what time her show aired and he absorbed every minute of it. "I'd cook recipes like napoleons and puff pastry and try the recipes out on the family maybe three or four times a year. They would suffer through them," he recalls. Eventually, he cooked his way through volumes I and II.

Many years later, Bayless was delighted by an invitation from his heroine and appeared on *In Julia's Kitchen with Master Chefs* television show. Bayless showcased a recipe for chile-glazed country ribs. He remembers, "I was scared to death," but she was her usual good-natured, engaging self, and put him completely at ease. He does a great impression of her enthusiastic trill.

More than twenty years after opening Frontera Grill, Bayless's affinity and talent for Mexican cooking is uncontested. He credits Americans' changing views about food and their embrace of all kinds of cultures for the nonstop success of his restaurants. His kitchens uplift the native Mexican cooking by avoiding the heavy-handed clichés, instead demonstrating the nuances inherent in Mexico's many regional cuisines.

Frontera Grill and Topolobampo both have received numerous awards and accolades, with Frontera honored as Outstanding Restaurant in America and Topolobampo twice nominated as Outstanding Restaurant in America by the James Beard Foundation. Altogether, Bayless has been earned eight different James Beard Foundation honors.

He closes the restaurants every summer for the Fourth of July holiday, taking his longtime crew on a field trip to Mexico. Thirty-five people made the trip in 2010. The group continues to learn and refine the details of Mexican regional cooking in its broad spectrum of tastes and flavors. "It keeps us fresh, we love the challenge, and it keeps getting better," he says of the crew. Many of his colleagues have been with him for the restaurant's twenty-three years in business. It's their personal fiesta time.

"We need to break the rhythms of our everyday lives, to plan and anticipate all the potential that a fiesta embraces. We need to experience those moments when time stands still—moments reached through the conduit of great food and drink," Bayless states. That is just how the Bayless family entertains at home on the weekends.

Like her father, the Bayless's daughter, Lanie, grew up in restaurants. She pitched in, greeting guests and pouring water, then as a teenager co-authored *Rick and Lanie's Excellent Kitchen Adventures* in 2006. The book combines the kitchen savvy and culinary escapades of a father and teenage daughter, traveling worldwide, meeting chefs, discovering markets, and experiencing exotic foods. Lanie is now majoring in theater at NYU, which seems natural to her parents, who believe that "the restaurant business is theater and good training."

In his best-selling cookbooks, Bayless takes complicated recipes and makes them user friendly. Notes on ingredients and techniques are carefully woven throughout and written with the same intensity that he puts into his restaurants.

"I TEND TO HAVE A LOT OF FOCUS, A LOT OF PASSION, WHEN I'M DOING SOMETHING," HE SAYS. "USUALLY I WORK ON ONE THING TO THE EXCLUSION OF EVERYTHING ELSE UNTIL I'M DONE."

The couple's sixth book, *Fiesta at Rick's: Fabulous Food, Luscious Libations, Great Times with Friends*, was published in 2010.

Bayless is not enamored of his celebrity status, and he knows that with it comes a social responsibility. He says, "I see that I have a role to play in our society and I can use it for good. So I take the stage that has been offered to me because it presents the opportunity to say things that a lot of people can hear. I want to use it to say that we can help improve the quality of our own lives and make this world a better place to live."

GREEN HERB CEVICHE *with* CUCUMBER *Ceviche Verde con Pepino*

HERB SEASONING

½ head garlic, cloves broken apart

2 or 3 fresh serrano chiles

1 medium bunch cilantro, thick bottom stems cut off (1 cup packed)

1 small bunch flat-leaf parsley, thick bottom stems cut off (1 cup packed)

½ cup olive oil

Salt

CEVICHE

¼ cup fresh lime juice, plus more if needed

1½ pounds sashimi-quality skinless, boneless fish fillets, such as Alaskan halibut, ahi tuna, or aqua-cultured Kona Kampachi, cut into ½-inch cubes

7 ounces small pickling cucumbers or Persian (baby) cucumbers, cut into ½-inch cubes

Salt, if needed

2 ripe large avocados, pitted, flesh scooped from skin and cut into cubes

Lettuce leaves, preferably butter lettuce, for garnish

To make the herb seasoning

1. Set a dry skillet over medium heat. Lay in the unpeeled garlic cloves and chiles. Roast, turning frequently, until they are soft and blotchy brown in spots, about 10 minutes for the chiles and 15 minutes for the garlic. Cool until easy to handle, and then slip the skins off the garlic, pull the stems off the chiles, and roughly chop (no need to remove the seeds). Put them in a food processor along with the cilantro, parsley, oil, and 2 generous teaspoons salt. Process until nearly smooth (it will be pasty). Scrape the mixture into a storage container and refrigerate until serving time.

To make the ceviche

1. In a large bowl, whisk together the lime juice and ½ cup of the herb seasoning. (Cover and refrigerate the remainder for another preparation.) Add the fish and cucumber, and stir to combine. To blend the flavors, cover and refrigerate for ½ hour (for best results, no more than 1 hour). Taste and season with a little more lime juice or salt if needed, then gently stir in the avocado (save a little for garnish if you want). Serve on plates or in martini glasses lined with lettuce leaves.

SERVES 6 TO 8 AS A STARTER

SMOKY PEANUT MOLE *with* GRILLED QUAIL
Cordonices Asadas en Mole de Cacahuate

PEANUT MOLE

2 medium (about 1 ounce total) dried ancho chiles, stemmed and seeded

2 tablespoons vegetable or olive oil

1/2 small white onion, sliced

2 garlic cloves, peeled

8 ounces ripe tomatoes

1 cup dry-roasted peanuts

2 slices firm white bread
(or 1/2 dry Mexican bolillo roll), torn into pieces

2 canned chipotle chiles in adobo sauce, seeded

1/2 teaspoon cinnamon, preferably freshly ground Mexican canela

1/8 teaspoon allspice, preferably freshly ground

3 1/2 cups chicken broth, plus more if needed

1/2 cup fruity red wine

1 tablespoon cider vinegar

2 bay leaves

Salt

Sugar

QUAIL

12 partially-boned quail, at least 4 ounces each

Vegetable or olive oil

Freshly ground black pepper

Chopped dry-roasted peanuts, for garnish

Sprigs of fresh flat-leaf parsley, for garnish

To make the peanut mole

1. Tear the ancho chiles into flat pieces, then toast a few at a time on an ungreased griddle or skillet over medium heat. Press the pieces flat with a metal spatula for a few seconds, until they crackle and change color slightly, then flip and press again. (If they give off more than the slightest wisp of smoke, they are burning and will add a bitter element to the sauce.) In a small bowl, cover the chiles with hot water and let them rehydrate for 30 minutes, stirring occasionally to ensure even soaking. Drain and discard the water.

2. Meanwhile, preheat the broiler. Heat 1 tablespoon of the oil in a heavy, 4-quart Dutch oven over medium heat. Add the onion and garlic, and fry, stirring regularly, until well browned, about 10 minutes. Scrape them into a blender jar. Set the pot aside.

3. Roast the tomatoes on a baking sheet 4 inches below the very hot broiler until blackened, about 5 minutes, then flip them and roast the other side; cool, then peel, collecting all the juice with the tomatoes. Add the tomatoes to the blender, along with the peanuts, bread, chipotles, drained anchos, cinnamon, and allspice. Add 1 1/2 cups of the broth and blend until smooth, stirring and scraping down the sides of the blender jar, and adding a little more liquid if needed to keep everything moving through the blades. Press the mixture through a medium-mesh strainer into a bowl.

4. Heat the remaining 1 tablespoon oil in the pot over medium-high heat. When hot enough to make a drop of the purée sizzle sharply, add all the purée at once. Stir as the nutty-smelling, ruddy-red mixture thickens and darkens for about 5 minutes, then stir in the remaining 2 cups broth, the wine, vinegar, and bay leaves. Partially cover and gently simmer over medium-low heat for roughly 45 minutes, stirring regularly for the flavors to harmonize. If necessary, thin the sauce with a little more broth to keep it the consistency of a cream soup. Taste and season with salt, usually about 1½ teaspoons, and about 1 tablespoon sugar. Cover and keep warm.

To make the quail

1. Thirty to 45 minutes before serving, light a gas grill or prepare a charcoal fire and let the coals burn until they are covered with gray ash and medium-hot. Position the grill grate about 8 inches above the coals and lightly oil it.

2. While the grill heats, lay the quail on a baking sheet. Tie the legs together with kitchen twine, then brush both sides with oil and sprinkle with salt and pepper.

3. Lay the quail on the hottest portion of the grill, breast-side down. Cover the grill and cook about 8 minutes, checking once or twice to ensure that they are not browning too quickly. Flip the quail and move to a cooler portion of the grill (quail finished over a cooler fire always seems juicier). Cover and continue grilling until the leg meat will separate from the bone quite easily when you squeeze a leg between two fingers, 4 to 6 minutes more.

4. Remove to a plate and keep warm in a low oven while you set up your plates. Ladle a generous ⅓ cup of the mole onto each of six warm dinner plates. Set 2 quail over the sauce on each plate. Garnish with chopped peanuts and sprigs of parsley.

NOTE: The mole may be made up to 5 days ahead. Cover and refrigerate. If oil separates from the sauce when reheated, either skim it off or blend the sauce in a loosely covered blender. The quail are best cooked just before serving.

SERVES 6

1996

JEREMIAH TOWER

CHAPTER *seven*

THERE COULD HARDLY HAVE BEEN A LESS LIKELY OR LESS QUALIFIED APPLICANT THAN JEREMIAH TOWER, WHO PRESENTED HIMSELF ONE DAY AT CHEZ PANISSE IN BERKELEY, CALIFORNIA, TO APPLY FOR THE CHEF'S JOB. He had a grandiose attitude and a Harvard master's degree in architecture, but no formal kitchen training.

Tower, born in Stamford, Connecticut, grew up traveling the world with his family. His father was director of an international sound equipment company. It wasn't an average childhood, and on one night at a rare family dinner at a London hotel, his parents glanced across the table at young Jeremiah and realized they'd forgotten to enroll him in school. He was eight at the time. After that tiny oversight, Tower's grandfather assumed responsibility for his education, seeing that he attended boarding schools in England, France, Australia, and the United States. Tower spent a lot of his childhood in posh hotels, on luxury ocean liners, and—perhaps most importantly—in the world's most celebrated restaurants, where he learned, as he says, "how things should taste. I have the advantage of an excellent flavor memory."

Those well-trained taste buds, paired with an appetite for adventure, earned him credit for helping to ignite the California culinary revolution of the 1970s.

In boarding school and college, Tower taught himself to cook, his mother and aunt having shown him the basics. Tower cites his earliest food memory as grilling a fresh-caught barracuda on a beach near the Great Barrier Reef in Australia with his aborigine pal. While in college and graduate school, he cooked his way though Escoffier's *Ma Cuisine*, making elaborate dinners for friends. Not until his grandfather died, when Jeremiah realized he needed to work, did he consider becoming a professional chef.

"I enjoyed cooking and, not being good at anything else except gardening, working at a restaurant made sense," he recalls. When he heard that James Beard was going to give classes in San Francisco at the Stanford Court Hotel, Tower, who was living in San Francisco, wrote to Beard and asked to attend the class.

"Arriving in my best togs—always Armani black label, Turnbull & Asser shirts, Charvet accessories—I was sufficiently a sight for him to pay immediate attention when I introduced myself," he says. "Since Beard never forgot a name, he remembered my letter." Two famous cookbook authors were also there, Barbara Kafka and Marion Cunningham. "Barbara was very sweet to me, but Marion was fiercely protective of Beard," Tower remembers.

After meeting Beard, Tower invited him to dinner at his home. He recounts, "I served sea urchin roe soufflé, each person getting a whole green urchin that I had cleaned out and used as a soufflé dish. He was overwhelmed. Those soufflés started a lifelong friendship."

"In 1972, I spent my last few dollars on a ride from San Francisco to Berkeley to answer an ad for a chef," Tower says. "I was told to return at a later time than scheduled; so, broke, I insisted right then on the interview. Alice [Waters] asked me to straighten out some soup—I think I added salt or cream—and she hired me on the spot. She must have been desperate, too." Tower's new job began a partnership of lusty affection and even lustier squabbling. Berkeley in the early 1970s was a hotbed of free love, lofty ideals, and political posturing, and Chez Panisse was a revolving door of characters. The guests held court every evening, and the staff weighed in with their own opinions. Tower, who had taken to making sweeping pronouncements when he'd enter the dining room, usually with a champagne glass in his hand, fit right in. Meanwhile in the kitchen, he kept Italian opera blasting—Puccini, Bellini, Rossini, and Verdi. The music was a fitting accompaniment to the daily drama of Chez Panisse.

Tower, who was still searching for his identity as a chef, brought focus and consistency to the menu by reviving recipes of the French masters like Escoffier and Fernand Point. After only a year as the restaurant's first chef, Tower was made a partner in the operation.

"At Chez Panisse, we got by on what we had available. Sometimes a friend would stop at the back door with a basket of tomatoes and trade it for a meal," Tower says. This practice spurred him to approach farmers and purveyors to supply fresh products, and that was his breakthrough. The daily changing menu, while French in style, began to emphasize locally grown, seasonal ingredients. Tower became a pivotal personality in the harmonic convergence that brought American restaurants and farmers together.

It was while Tower was there that Chez Panisse earned its national and international acclaim. In October 1975, *Gourmet* magazine reviewed the restaurant, praising Tower for "joyously exploring *la vraie cuisine française*, in all its vigor, freshness, and variety."

Eventually, though, Tower decided he had exhausted all the regions in France, and all the French cookbook authors whose recipes interested him. On October 7, 1976, he served a "Northern California Regional Dinner." The menu listed the farmers, ranchers, and fishmongers of the Bay Area whose products appeared on the menu: Spenger's Tomales Blue Point Oysters, Big Sur Garrapata Creek Smoked Trout, Monterey Bay Prawns, and Preserved California Geese from Sebastopol.

"We brought these live trout up from Garrapata Trout Farm in Big Sur in tanks, and had bathtubs and pails all over the kitchen with compressors putting air into the water," Tower says. "Every time there was an order, I'd grab a trout and kill it and shove it into the court bouillon, but the first trout slipped out of my fingers and went flopping across the floor just as a waiter was coming into the kitchen. It flopped out into the dining room and ended up on some dowager's ankles, then there were shrieks all over the restaurant, and that really made the evening. Everyone came piling into the kitchen to see what we were doing. That's when I knew that theater was at least half the story."

Tower went to great lengths to get the choicest ingredients, striking deals with local California farmers. In an interview, one of Tower's early sous-chefs, Willy Bishop, recalls, "Generally it worked, and it worked because this guy, Jeremiah, was so manic and insane. If he was gonna make bouillabaisse, he'd go to Chinatown and come back with, like, a six-foot conger eel. 'Look what I got in Chinatown!' I was like, 'What the hell is it?'"

As Tower remembers, "At a butcher's place, I'd get shoulder deep into drums filled with calves' livers and just stand there with a pail, grabbing the livers as they went by. I wanted the blond ones, so I had to roll up my sleeves and dig in there in order to find them. The blond livers are milder, you see, closer to foie gras. The people who worked there thought I was crazy, and of course I was."

In 1978, Tower sold his shares and left Chez Panisse, passing the job to his sous-chef, Jean-Pierre Moullé. After teaching cooking classes and working at other restaurants in California, Tower opened Stars in San Francisco. Attracted by the handsome chef, his cuisine, and his bad-boy panache, celebrities and socialites packed the restaurant nightly, making it one of the hippest spots in San Francisco. Often seen roaring through the city on a fire engine–red motorcycle, Tower would take breaks from Stars at Zuni Café, his local hang-out, where a glass of champagne would be waiting on the bar as soon as the staff heard the motorcycle scream to a halt.

"I love the guy!" says Chef Mario Batali, who worked at Stars with Tower. "He's a culinary inspiration." Tower and Batali share a tendency to mask professional fortitude behind expansive public personalities, but Tower influenced Batali's taste for bright flavors, grand aspirations, and perhaps his current mode of transportation. Batali zips around Manhattan on his own two wheels, a Vespa. Other Tower protégées and members of the opening Stars team include Emily Luchetti, now executive pastry chef at Farallon and Waterbar, and Mark Franz, owner and executive chef of Farallon, Waterbar, and Nick's Cove.

"I don't think many people see beyond Tower as 'the chef,'" says Steven Vranian, another Stars alumnus. "He once told me that the hardest thing he ever did was to take off the chef's coat and put on his Armani. We all hid behind that white coat, but Tower was first a restaurateur; he worked all of Stars: bartender, maître d', wine buyer and steward, cook and, of course, as architect, designing the restaurants and constantly changing them. He was a hands-on operator who planned all the marketing and publicity. He taught all of us—at least those who listened—the importance of hospitality, from the feel of a napkin to the weight of a fork and wine glass to the color, lighting, and vision of a room. Every detail had to be right."

Tower notes that California cuisine would never have been labeled as such if not for a few French chefs whose pushiness brought out his competitive side. At a 1983 event in Rhode Island called "Innovations," designed to spotlight cranberries, Tower pulled out the histrionics: "Guy Savoy, who was the Young Turk in France at the time, was invited to come to the United States and put on a dinner for a hundred American food journalists so they could see what the so-called Nouvelle Cuisine in France was really like. Then they invited some of us California kids to do a funny little lunch to keep everybody's strength up. We got to the Astor mansion and we were in the kitchen, and of course the French arrived and said, 'Out, out, out!' Obviously, they were the important ones, and they wanted the kitchen. So, I looked around for a place to cook, and remembered that idea of theater. The only heat source we had was two six-foot-long grills, and mesquite charcoal. We set the grills and tables right in front of where the journalists were going to have lunch. Staging is everything. We cooked it all there. It was the first time they had ever seen grilling and salsas, and things like that. And it fired their imaginations. It was certainly the first time we'd ever cooked dessert on a charcoal grill."

Tower tells how he cooked fruit ragout for dessert, and that the crowd loved the sight of six chefs, each with a sauté pan in his hand, tossing together in sequence. "We stole the show and kidnapped the media coverage," Tower says triumphantly.

"THE TERM 'CALIFORNIA CUISINE' WAS BORN, AND WHAT THAT MEANT WAS PLASTERED ACROSS EVERY NEWSPAPER FOOD SECTION IN AMERICA. IT WAS A DELICIOUS FEELING."

"On the trip back after the Astor mansion event, I was stunned into a coma. All I could think was, 'What have I done?' The life I knew before was over, and now I was riding a white shark that needed to be fed every week in the food sections. So I decided to wear spurs, and get on with it," he says.

Tower says that the enthusiasm for fresh ingredients generated by the California cuisine movement in the 1970s and 1980s changed American cuisine forever. "You can get boutique farm and baby vegetables and lettuces and wild rice and fresh herbs pretty much everywhere now. What's left for chefs to work with, in terms of innovation? Does that raise the bar?" he asks.

In Tower's opinion, it does raise the bar. But the challenge now is not to find the ingredients, though that is, he believes, still a huge part of any chef's work. He thinks the challenge is to step back and let the food and ingredients really speak, rather than say "Look, that is the food of a famous chef." It's not necessarily doing something new, but doing something new for yourself, and letting the food be famous.

After owning several restaurants (Stars, Stars Café, Singapore Stars, Seattle Stars, Speedo 690, and The Peak Café in Hong Kong), serving thousands of meals, and earning national recognition, Tower was named James Beard Foundation 1996 Outstanding Chef. In 1998, Tower sold the Stars group and closed others of his restaurants.

Now a writer more than a chef, Tower has written several books and regularly contributes to international culinary magazines. His first book, *New American Classics*, won a James Beard Foundation award in 1987 for Best American Regional Cookbook. His 2004 memoir, *California Dish: What I Saw (and Cooked) at the American Culinary Revolution*, detailing his participation in that movement, is a ribald, controversial account of California cuisine's high jinks and low moments.

Today, Tower has come full circle, using his degree in architecture to restore old colonial mansions in Merida, Mexico, and working on a land development project near Chichén Itzá. He regularly goes scuba diving with sharks frolicking nearby. "They're friendlier there than in a restaurant," he says with characteristic flair.

CHILLED HONEYDEW MELON SOUP *with* CRAB RÉMOULADE

MELON SOUP

1 large, fresh basil sprig

¼ habañero chile, seeded

Pinch ground cumin

2 cups 1-inch dice honeydew melon

2 tablespoons plain yogurt

Salt

CRAB RÉMOULADE

1 cup mayonnaise

1 tablespoon Creole mustard

1 tablespoon minced fresh flat-leaf parsley

1 tablespoon minced fresh tarragon

1 tablespoon grated white onion

1 lemon, zested

2 teaspoons hot sauce

1 teaspoon smoked paprika (pimentón)

2 cups lump crabmeat, picked over

Fresh chervil leaves

Hot sauce

Nasturtium or other edible flowers, shredded (optional)

To make the soup

1. In a 1-quart saucepan over high heat, bring ½ cup water to a boil. Add the basil, chile, and cumin. Simmer for 5 minutes. Strain and discard the seasonings, reserving the water. In a food processor or blender, purée half of the melon and half of the seasoned water. Press the purée through a strainer or *chinois* into a medium bowl. Repeat with the remaining melon and water. Stir the yogurt into the melon mixture. Season with salt, cover, and refrigerate the soup for at least 2 hours.

To make the rémoulade

1. In a large bowl, whisk together the mayonnaise, mustard, parsley, tarragon, onion, zest, hot sauce, and paprika. Cover and refrigerate for at least 2 hours.

2. Immediately prior to serving, fold the crabmeat into the rémoulade. Pour the melon soup into chilled soup plates. Mound crab in the center of each. Garnish with chervil, hot sauce, and edible flowers, if using.

SERVES 6 TO 8

POACHED CHICKEN BREASTS *with* HOMINY *and* CRAYFISH

CRAYFISH TAILS AND SAUCE

2 tablespoons olive oil

24 whole, live crayfish

1 teaspoon paprika

2 sprigs fresh thyme

¼ cup chardonnay or muscadet

2 large tomatoes, seeded, coarsely chopped

1 cup clam stock or other rich fish or shellfish stock

2 sprigs fresh flat-leaf parsley

4 to 6 tablespoons unsalted butter

Salt

Freshly ground black pepper

CHICKEN BREASTS

4 large skin-on chicken breasts with first wing-bone

2 tablespoons butter

2 sprigs fresh tarragon

4 garlic cloves, unpeeled, coarsely chopped

2 cups chicken stock

4 leaves green Swiss chard, stems removed

1 cup cooked white hominy, drained and rinsed

1 cup cooked yellow hominy, drained and rinsed

To make the tails and sauce

1. Heat the oil in a 12-inch stockpot over medium heat. Add the crayfish, paprika, and thyme and stir constantly for 3 minutes. Add the wine and stir to scrape up the browned bits from the bottom of the pot. Add the tomatoes, stock, and parsley. Simmer until the crayfish tails are almost cooked, 2 to 3 minutes.

2. Remove the crayfish and set aside to cool, reserving the cooking liquid. Peel the crayfish and save the tail meat separately. Place the heads and shells in a food processor with the cooking liquid and purée. Strain the liquid into a 2-quart saucepan. Cook it over medium heat to reduce the volume if there is more than 3/4 cup. Whisk in the butter and correct the seasoning with salt and pepper as necessary.

To make the chicken

1. Cut the wing bones from the breasts. Melt the butter over medium heat in a 12-inch sauté pan. Add the tarragon and garlic. Stir over medium heat for 2 minutes. Season the breasts and wings with salt and pepper and place them skin-side down in the sauté pan. Cook for 2 minutes and turn over, cooking for another 2 minutes. Add the stock, bring to a simmer, cover, and poach until the breasts are half cooked, about 5 minutes longer.

2. Remove the chicken and reserve the poaching liquid. When the chicken is cool enough to handle, remove and discard the skin. Set the chicken aside.

3. Strain the poaching liquid, skim to remove any fat, and return the poaching liquid to the sauté pan. Add the chard and simmer for 5 minutes, or until soft enough to fold around the chicken but still very green in color. Remove the chard and set aside. Reserve half of the cooking liquid in the sauté pan. Add the white and yellow hominy and cook over low heat for 10 minutes. Season with salt and pepper.

4. Wrap a chard leaf around each breast. Place the wrapped breasts and the wings back in the sauté pan on top of the hominy and liquid. Cover and finish cooking, 5 to 7 minutes.

5. Using a slotted spoon, place the hominy without any liquid onto warmed plates and set the wrapped breasts in the center. Add the wing bone to the plate. Spoon the crayfish sauce and crayfish tail meat around the chicken and serve.

NOTE: Crayfish tails and seafood stock reduced by half may be substituted for whole live crayfish and shell purée, but the dish will lack the intensity of flavor imparted by the shell purée.

SERVES 4

1997

THOMAS KELLER

CHAPTER *eight*

THOMAS KELLER IS OFTEN SPOKEN OF IN HUSHED TONES, MINIMAL ADJECTIVES, AND SPARSE ADVERBS. But there's the real guy, a long, tall drink of water, lanky in faded jeans with an off-in-the-distance stare, who ought to be called Tommy.

Is it possible to be such a buttoned-up king of the kitchen and—at the same time—wear cowboy boots when he relaxes? Perhaps this is what you call an enigma—another word that's been used to describe Thomas Keller. Those who know him say Keller's reserve isn't shyness; it's more about contemplation. They say that lurking beneath his zeal for routine, for procedure, there's a considerate, funny guy. They also understand that he's a force of nature. And they don't mean it dismissively. A staff member explains, "Cooking's his life. His entire life. Other people go to work, go home. Thomas lives the whole experience."

About an hour and a half north of San Francisco, in the town of Yountville, in the Napa Valley, is a sanctuary—a food sanctuary called The French Laundry. Some will tell you it's the best restaurant in America. Some will tell you Thomas Keller is the best chef in America. What Keller believes is that great cooking comes from the heart. His heart came to the stove young. As a boy, Keller, the fifth of six children, was expected to help his mother, who held a variety of restaurant jobs.

As Keller remembers, "My parents were divorced. My mother didn't have a babysitter, so I'd go to the restaurant where she worked and wash dishes."

One night, standing at that sink, young Keller had an epiphany: He enjoyed the repetition of turning a dirty dish into a clean one. "Repetition and rituals are important to me. Specific times. Specific days. Repetition is how someone becomes good at something. Do it over and over again," he says.

Even today, methodical systems unify Keller's cooking, his restaurant, and his staff, who are trained and tested, and reflect on their performance after every service. He hired a choreographer to train the dining room staff to perform their functions with a complimentary grace and symmetry. For the guests, the table's aura, "the bubble," is never to be burst. No detail is overlooked.

He didn't always have these rules. In the beginning, Keller was just another kid with a job in a kitchen. It was when he worked summers at the Palm Beach Yacht Club that Keller first discovered he liked to cook better than he *liked* washing dishes—and he really liked washing dishes.

In 1976, Roland Henin hired him to cook the staff's meals at The Dunes Club in Rhode Island. Even today, Thomas Keller still calls Roland Henin "my chef." Henin taught Keller how a professional kitchen works, how a chef works, and how it all comes together. Henin loaned Keller a copy of Fernand Point's *Ma Gastronomie*, which was pivotal for Keller. Years later, he was honored to write the foreword to a new addition of the book.

Over the years, Keller moved from kitchen to kitchen, learning, succeeding, failing, and then succeeding again. He traveled to France where he added Guy Savoy, Le Pres Catalan, and Taillevent, all Michelin-starred houses, to his resume before returning to New York. Successful runs at La Reserve and Restaurant Raphael in New York led to Rakel, opened in 1986 by Keller and his partner, Serge Raoul. Rakel was the best neighborhood restaurant in New York until the economy dived. Out of work, he headed to California to look for a job and a little consulting work.

In the back of his mind was a vision: A special place, small, in an idyllic setting, like some of those he had seen in the French countryside. Perhaps a place with climbing roses.

In time, he came across a building in Yountville, California. The ivy-covered structure looked more like a house than a restaurant, which it had become after it was a saloon, a brothel, and a French steam laundry. Later, in his best-selling *The French Laundry Cookbook*, Keller noted, "It seemed as if I'd been heading there my whole working life." He approached the couple who were running it—mayor Don Schmitt, and his wife Sally—and arranged to buy it.

It took eighteen months of hard work to turn the former laundry building into The French Laundry, the restaurant he envisioned.

"My biggest asset was my total ignorance. If someone had told me, 'Thomas, you are going to be working on this for the next eighteen months. You will have to get a small business loan. You'll have to talk to four hundred people to get money' and do all these things I couldn't do, I would not have believed them," Keller says.

However, shortly after The French Laundry opened in 1994, Ruth Reichl reviewed it in the *New York Times*: "Imagine a restaurant hidden in the middle of the vineyards. It is an old stone house filled with the golden light of many candles. There is a courtyard in the center, and on fine nights, tables are set in the fragrant garden beneath a starry sky. We're dreaming here, so picture each meal as a series of small fantastic tastes, served at a leisurely pace by waiters who want nothing but your happiness. They search your face, watching as flavors you could never have conceived flit across your palate, willing you to like each one."

Keller's life, The French Laundry, and Yountville were never the same.

The restaurant became a destination for people who consider food a serious subject—serious enough to plan far in advance. One does not drop in for a bite at The French Laundry on the spur of the moment. Nor, once there, does one eat and run.

A meal at The French Laundry is a tasting of many small, intensely flavored dishes with no ingredient repeated. Components are designed to excite the imagination and pique curiosity; the dishes are matched with wines to best exhilarate the palate. The meal can stretch for hours.

"I really believe in the law of diminishing returns," says Keller. After three or four bites, taste peaks. So, he gives you a few perfect bites and leaves you wanting another just as the waiter puts the next dish down in front of you. "When your guest says, 'God, I wish I had one more bite....' That's what we're trying to achieve," he says. "That's our goal; our philosophy."

Whimsy is another part of the philosophy. "Oysters and Pearls," one of his famous flavor combinations, came about when he noticed a box of tapioca pearls on a grocery shelf. Pearls come from oysters. Tapioca looks like pearls. This mental leapfrogging became Sabayon of Pearl Tapioca with Island Creek Oysters and White Sturgeon Caviar.

He also created a delicious little serendipity of taste with his now-famous takeoff on ice cream cones: Tiny cornets filled with crème fraîche, topped with a perfect scoop of salmon tartare. You get your cone at the beginning of the meal, not the end. He uses fanciful culinary twists on other menu items, but Keller is playful only when he's certain that it works, that it will bring a new dimension to the table—and maybe a smile.

"I LOVE TO HEAR SOMEONE SAY, 'THIS REMINDS ME OF . . . ,' AND THEN THEY TELL ME ABOUT A WONDERFUL EXPERIENCE THAT THEY HAD SOMEWHERE," SAYS KELLER. "I HOPE THEY GO SOMEWHERE ELSE NOW AND SAY, 'THIS REMINDS ME OF THE FRENCH LAUNDRY.' BECAUSE IT'S THOSE MEMORIES THAT I THINK ARE THE MOST IMPORTANT."

Does Keller go to extremes? Is he too methodical, too precise, too obsessed with perfection? The word he chooses is "finesse." In fact, a sign over the kitchen door reminds staff that finesse is "refinement and delicacy of performance, execution or artisanship."

Michael Ruhlman, Keller's friend and the acclaimed author who worked closely with Keller to produce four award-winning cookbooks, says Keller is "incredibly, uncommonly thoughtful" about his work and the people around him. "He always challenges everyone. The idea is that if you approach every day like that you'll get very good at what you're doing. He helped me to see in the kitchen—he taught me how to pay attention, how to be observant—aware that if a pot of cream boils over, you not only have a mess; you no longer have enough cream. When I asked why he was removing the membrane from a side of tuna, he asked me to taste the membrane. That taught me why he was removing it."

But while he creates haute cuisine, Keller also has a taste for simple things: roast chicken, peanut butter, pizza, and the instant oatmeal he usually enjoys for breakfast. Hot dogs were a staple of his childhood, he still welcomes the sight of a taco truck, and he laughs when he recalls that he once toyed with the notion of opening a hamburger stand.

In addition to The French Laundry, Keller's Yountville restaurants now include Bouchon Bistro, Bouchon Bakery, and Ad Hoc, a family-style restaurant; and there's a three-acre kitchen garden. "We opened Bouchon because we needed a place to eat," recalls Keller. "Everything was closed by 9:30 at night. We were wide awake after work and wanted to go eat—we didn't want to just go to bed." The bakery was opened so that The French Laundry would have its own bread, but has grown to encompass its own retail and wholesale operation.

"The idea for Ad Hoc came up with everyone sitting around the table on April 1. No kidding. Everyone else thought it was an April Fool's joke when an e-mail went out that night to the team," he says. "It was supposed to be temporary so it was named Ad Hoc, which literally means, 'for this purpose.'"

Keller, like most great chefs, is happy to pass along what he's learned. Grant Achatz, chef/owner of Alinea in Chicago, was young and inexperienced when Keller hired him. "It was 1996, so I was only twenty-two, and really needed a strong leader," says Achatz. "I needed somebody to guide me, not only in cooking, but learning restaurants. Ultimately, he instilled a set of values that went beyond the kitchen and into my life. He was the first one in the door and the last one to leave. He was twenty years older than all of his cooks and outworking them by far. And I watched him become more and more successful, by hard work." Achatz learned well. The James Beard Foundation named him Outstanding Chef in 2008.

In 2004, Keller turned his focus toward opening the restaurant Per Se, an urban interpretation of The French Laundry in the middle of Manhattan. The name came about because Keller had to repeatedly explain that the restaurant wouldn't be The French Laundry, per se. Now some critics have called both restaurants the best in America. Also that year came Keller's business expansion to Las Vegas with a second Bouchon. Bouchon Bakery opened there in 2004 and in New York's Time Warner Center in 2006, with a third New York location scheduled to open in 2011. Keller, now a businessman, and always an honest man, explains exactly what that means in his world. "I'm not solely a chef any longer—I have become a restaurateur."

There is a difference. "My life changed a lot," says Keller. "I was all of a sudden out of my spot in the kitchen. I don't stand there expediting anymore—because I can't." Keller loves the idea of what he's doing in his new role, though. "Impacting this team and how they will impact others. It's a great thing even though I still struggle with not being the chef and working in the kitchen, having those wonderful moments with the team. It makes you feel a little older because you are not in there, but at the same time you have to realize that you can't work sixteen hours a day forever," he says.

Despite all the acclaim, Keller tries to keep a realistic perspective: "It's great to be the first American ever to have seven Michelin stars. It's great to be the first American to have two simultaneous Michelin three-star ratings. The first to win back-to-back James Beard awards. All these firsts, but what I've accomplished has to do with so many people."

Next door to The French Laundry, a bungalow called the Bocuse House serves as a small test kitchen and harbors occasional chef-friends, among them Paul Bocuse himself. Inside the little kitchen, Keller kicks off his clogs and slides around in socks to music, regularly wiping up footprints tracked in when vegetables are carried in from the garden across the road.

That's Thomas Keller, too.

CAVIAR *with* BRIOCHE *and* AVOCADO MOUSSE

BRIOCHE

⅓ cup very warm water (110° to 115°F)

One ¼-ounce package active dry yeast (not quick-rising)

2⅓ cups cake flour

2 cups all-purpose flour

⅓ cup sugar

2½ teaspoons fine sea salt

6 large eggs, at room temperature

1¼ cups unsalted butter, at room temperature, diced into 1-inch cubes, plus butter for the pans

AVOCADO MOUSSE

3½ ounces peeled, pitted avocado

1 tablespoon plus 1 teaspoon crème fraîche

½ teaspoon pistachio oil

Pinch ascorbic acid

Salt

6 to 8 ounces caviar

To make the brioche

1. Combine the water and yeast in a small glass bowl; let rest for 10 minutes. Stir with a non-metallic spoon until the yeast is completely dissolved.

2. Sift the cake flour, all-purpose flour, sugar, and salt into the bowl of a stand mixer fitted with a dough hook. Add the eggs and beat for 1 minute at low speed, scraping down the sides with a rubber spatula as needed. Slowly add the dissolved yeast and continue beating at low speed for 5 minutes. Stop the mixer and scrape any dough off the dough hook, then resume beating for another 5 minutes. Add one fourth of the butter cubes and beat for 1 minute. Continue to add the butter in fourths, beating for 1 minute for each addition. Once all the butter is added, beat for 10 to 15 minutes longer, until the dough is smooth.

3. Remove the dough from the mixer and place it in a large, floured mixing bowl. Cover and set aside in a warm place until doubled in size, about 3 hours.

4. Turn the dough out onto a generously floured work surface and gently work the air bubbles out by folding the dough over several times while lightly pressing down on it. Return the dough to the bowl, cover, and refrigerate overnight.

5. Generously butter two 8½-by-4½-by-3-inch loaf pans. Turn the dough out onto a floured work surface. With floured hands, divide it in half and shape into two rectangles to fit the loaf pans. Place the dough in the pans. Let them rise, uncovered, in a warm place until ½ inch above the top of pans, about 3 hours.

6. Preheat the oven to 350°F.

7. Bake the brioche until well browned on top and the loaves sound hollow when tapped on the bottom, 35 to 40 minutes. Remove from the oven and immediately turn the loaves out onto a wire rack. Let cool for 10 minutes.

8. If serving within a few hours, promptly wrap the hot bread in aluminum foil and store at room temperature until ready to use. If freezing, immediately wrap the hot bread in foil and promptly freeze for up to 1 month. (If frozen, when ready to use, reheat while still wrapped in foil and without thawing at 250°F for 20 to 25 minutes.)

To make the avocado mousse

1. Combine the avocado, crème fraîche, oil, ascorbic acid, and a pinch of salt in a blender and blend until smooth. Press through a *chinois*. Put the mousse in a pastry bag and refrigerate. Reserve.

2. To make brioche rounds, preheat the oven to 300°F. Cut three or four 1/8-inch-thick slices from a brioche loaf. Using a 1-inch round cookie cutter, cut out 6 to 8 rounds. Place the rounds on a parchment paper–lined baking sheet. Place a second sheet of parchment on top of the rounds and set a second baking sheet atop the rounds to flatten them. Bake until golden brown, about 10 minutes.

To assemble

1. Place a 1-inch dollop of avocado mousse (about 1 tablespoon) in the center of each serving plate. Place 1 brioche round on top of the mousse. Add 1 ounce of caviar on top of the brioche round and serve.

NOTE: If you like, instead of making your own brioche, you can use good-quality freshly baked store-bought brioche. Better yet, use brioche from Bouchon Bakery if there is one near you.

SERVES 6 TO 8

LAMB *with* SWISS CHARD, TOKYO TURNIP, ARROWLEAF SPINACH, *and* DIJON MUSTARD MOUSSELINE

LAMB SHORT RIBS

16 lamb ribs, reserved from cutting lamb rib-eyes

Salt

Freshly ground black pepper

Canola oil

2 carrots, cut crosswise into 1-inch slices

2 onions, cut crosswise into 1-inch slices

2 leeks, cut crosswise into 1-inch slices

1 head garlic, cut in half lengthwise

1 bay leaf

1 bunch fresh thyme

1 bunch fresh parsley stems

6½ quarts lamb stock

SWISS CHARD RIBS

3 bouquet garnis of 1 bay leaf, 1 sprig thyme

1 clove garlic

2 teaspoons olive oil

Kosher salt

3 Cryovac bags

3 large red rainbow chard stems, cut 2½ inches by ½ inch

Olive oil

Champagne vinegar

SPINACH

4 ounces fresh spinach

1 Cryovac bag

3 tablespoons kosher salt

1 tablespoon olive oil, plus more for reheating

MOUSSELINE

6 egg yolks

½ cup clarified butter

2½ ounces heavy cream

1½ ounces mustard

1 tablespoon champagne vinegar

SAUCE D'AGNEAU

½ cup canola oil

1½ pounds lamb bones, chopped into 1-inch pieces

2½ cups strained chicken stock

1 cup ½-inch dice onions

1 cup ½-inch dice leeks

1 cup ½-inch dice carrots

½ ounce fresh thyme sprigs

2 garlic cloves, crushed

1 cup chopped tomatoes

1 cup veal stock

1 cup lamb stock

GLAZED TURNIPS

12 to 15 baby turnips, peeled

1 teaspoon sugar

LAMB LOINS

Olive oil

4 lamb loins, bias cut into 8 medallions, about 2 ounces per medallion

CONTINUED

To make the short ribs

1. Preheat the oven to 350°F. On the side of the ribs closest to the shoulder, count four bones and cut each section off. Season with salt and pepper.

2. Heat some oil in a large, shallow casserole over medium heat. Brown the ribs and then remove them. Pour out the excess oil and reduce the heat to low. Sweat the carrots, onions, leeks, garlic, bay leaf, thyme, and parsley stems by cooking until they soften but don't brown, about 3 minutes.

3. Return the ribs to the casserole and stack them so they will be easily removed later. Cover the contents with the lamb stock and bring to a simmer. Press parchment paper down on the surface and cover tightly with aluminum foil. Place in the oven and braise for approximately 2 hours. The ribs are done when the meat easily pulls away from the bone.

4. Allow the ribs to cool in the stock for 3 hours, then gently remove the ribs and allow them to continue cooling on a parchment paper–lined baking sheet.

5. If you're right-handed, hold the ribs in your left hand with the chine bone facing away from you. With your right thumb and index finger, grasp the bottom of the chine bone. Gently twist the bone and push forward to remove, taking care not to tear the meat.

6. Lay the deboned rib on a fresh parchment paper–lined baking sheet with the meat-side down, being sure to remove any clinging mirepoix. Season with salt and pepper. Lay a second piece of parchment paper on top of the ribs and then another baking sheet. Weight the top tray to press the ribs; refrigerate overnight.

To make the Swiss chard ribs

1. Add 1 bouquet garni to each Cryovac bag. Set vacuum-pack level on medium high. Cook in a sous vide at 185°F for 25 minutes. Place each bag in an ice bath to chill completely. In a small sauté pan over medium heat, warm the stems in a drizzle of olive oil, a few drops of champagne vinegar, and a pinch of salt and white pepper.

To make the spinach

1. Put the spinach in the Cryovac bag with the salt and oil. Set vacuum level on medium high for at least 5 minutes. To reheat, put in medium sauté pan over low heat with olive oil.

To make the mousseline

1. In a large bowl, whisk together the egg yolks, butter, cream, mustard, vinegar, and 1 tablespoon water until creamy. Season with salt and pepper. Place the mixture into a whipped cream dispenser. Close tightly and fill the canister with two nitrous oxide charges one at a time. Set aside.

To make the sauce d'agneau

1. Heat the oil over high heat in a wide, heavy pot that is large enough to hold the bones in one layer. When the oil begins to smoke, add the bones. Sear the bones without stirring for about 10 minutes. Turn the bones and cook for 10 minutes more, or until evenly colored.

2. For the first deglazing, add 1 cup water to the pot. Stirring with a wooden spoon, scrape up any glazed juices that cling to the bottom of the pot and cook until the liquid has evaporated and the pot is reglazed and sizzling again. For the second deglazing, add half of the chicken stock and allow it to boil down. For the third deglazing, add onions, leeks, and carrots and cook until the moisture has evaporated and the vegetables are lightly caramelized. Add the thyme and garlic and cook until the juices evaporate to form another glaze. For the fourth deglazing, add the tomatoes and cook until the juices evaporate and form another glaze. For the fifth deglazing, add the remaining chicken stock, the veal stock, and the lamb stock. Deglaze the pot and transfer the stock and bones into a smaller, narrower pot so that it will be easier to skim.

3. With the pot set partially off the burner to force impurities to one side, bring to a simmer and ladle off fat as it rises to the top. Simmer for another 30 to 45 minutes, skimming often, until the stock has reduced to the level of the bones. Strain through a china-cap sieve and then again through a *chinois*. Do not force any solids through the strainer or they will cloud the sauce. Pour the liquid into a small pot; reduce to about 1 cup and strain. Chill the sauce for use later or keep warm for immediate use.

To make the turnips

1. In a 1-quart saucepan over medium heat, combine the turnips, 2 cups water, the sugar, and a pinch of salt. Bring to a simmer and cook for 10 to 15 minutes, or until tender. Remove from the heat and set aside.

To make the lamb loins

1. In a 10-inch sauté pan over high heat, warm the oil and sear the loins on both sides. Continue cooking on each side until medium-rare, another 3 minutes. Rest 8 to 10 minutes and reserve warm.

To plate the lamb loins

1. In a 10-inch sauté pan, heat the Swiss chard ribs, turnips, and spinach until warm, 2 to 3 minutes. Place 2 pieces of the warmed lamb ribs in the center of the plate. Place 2 medallions of lamb loin next to the riblets. Place 2 small piles of the warmed spinach next to each of the lamb ribs. Add the Swiss chard ribs and glazed turnips. Ladle 1 ounce of sauce d'agneau around the plate and finish with a dollop of mousseline.

SERVES 6

1998

JEAN-GEORGES VONGERICHTEN

CHAPTER *nine*

"HE'S WORTH NOTHING." WITH THAT EVALUATION, JEAN-GEORGES VONGERICHTEN WAS KICKED OUT OF TECHNICAL SCHOOL. His parents expected him to join the family coal business in Strasbourg, France, but he admits "I had no passion for it. If you don't have a passion for what you're doing, drop it." Instead, Vongerichten dropped into a kitchen.

Now the head of international restaurant companies from America to Asia, Vongerichten doesn't feel too guilty that he abandoned the family business because he knew his younger brothers would join it. Feeding forty or fifty employees every day was much more to his liking.

For his sixteenth birthday, Vongerichten's parents took him to the Michelin three-star Auberge de l'Ill. Enthralled by the experience, when chef Paul Haeberlin came over to the table, Vongerichten had an epiphany. "I was amazed. I thought, 'This is it,'" he recalls.

Haeberlin soon found a place for the new apprentice—one that lasted three years and included a shift as *chiens chef*, or cooking for customers' dogs. The aspiring chef did his army service, then wrangled a position as a *commis*, a beginning cook, at Louis Outhier's three-star Michelin restaurant, l'Oasis, in La Napoule, close to Cannes.

"Outhier was a fanatic for cleanliness and order," Vongerichten remembers, a trait he passed on to the young chef, who modeled his personal style on his mentor's. He was a "very elegant, beautifully dressed, and very civilized man—a bit of a playboy. He taught me about clothes and about women as kind of a father figure to me."

Vongerichten next did a nine-month stint with Paul Bocuse, the famous Lyonnaise three-star chef, "I was a *commis*, young, still cooking at the stove. Every morning we went to the market, selecting great products. We would go through ten cases of tomatoes to pick the right one. Good food, but a bit like the army. Bocuse's kitchen is disciplined, hygienic. He insisted that we know how to clean, wash our hands every time we did something. He taught us how to become chefs. It was like the way my mother made me clean my room, and make the bed. It's good for kids. Teach them to pick up," remembers Vongerichten.

Outhier, who had a contract with the Mandarin Oriental hotel chain, offered Jean-Georges a job in Bangkok. In November 1980, the twenty-three-year-old Vongerichten took over a kitchen with a staff of twenty Thai cooks. While Vongerichten was cooking classical French food, he was falling in love with the flavors of Thailand. He stayed in Bangkok for two years before moving on to Singapore, Hong Kong, and Osaka, absorbing the local cuisine at each stop. He went from cooking with cream and butter to using ginger, lemongrass, and chiles. Vongerichten developed a love for the exotic and aromatic flavors of the East. "It changed the way I cook today; it changed my palate completely. I like to say that it's like alchemy," the chef remarks. Basing recipes on the French fundamentals of *au fond*, *bouillon*, *fumet*, and *jus*, he seeks sweetness, sourness, and bitterness in fruits and herbs and then finds additional *umami* in flavors from Asian cuisines.

His philosophy is all about creating cravings. People become comfortable with a couple of items on the menu in a particular restaurant, so he keeps those favorites on the menu all the time. "People come back for the foods that they are comfortable with. Then many people," he observes, "especially in New York City, want new items on the menu when they revisit my restaurants." At the same time, he's sensitive to the various shifts and appetites of his guests. "Seasonings are magical—vibrant. When people say, 'I never tasted this before!' then I know they get it, and this is what pushes me. That's my drive!"

In 1986, Vongerichten was twenty-eight-years old and got another assignment from Outhier—to start a dining room at the Drake Hotel on Park Avenue and 56th Street. New York in the 1980s was a heady time for the restaurant scene. The superstar chefs of the future were just gaining traction. David Bouley had left Montrachet and opened his own place, Daniel Boulud was at Le Cirque, and Thomas Keller was at Rakel. "It was a lot of pressure," Vongerichten says. "I'm a guy who always questions myself. Every day the bar was higher." But despite the pressure—or perhaps because of it—Vongerichten began making a name for himself.

"I was doing Outhier's style of cooking," he recalls. "For the first six months, I didn't leave the hotel. I was scared. I was a country boy. Then Gilbert le Coze came in. He took me to the Fulton Fish Market." Vongerichten then visited Chinatown, and was reunited with many of his favorite Asian ingredients. Within a year of arriving in New York, Jean-Georges was cooking food unlike anywhere else in Manhattan—or in the world.

Ready for equity or a new venture, Vongerichten teamed up with one of his most loyal customers, Phil Suarez, to find a space, an old pick-up joint on 64th Street. They signed the lease on January 25, 1991, just as the first Gulf War started and the recession deepened. Vongerichten was sleeping on a friend's foldout couch in a studio apartment as he prepared to open JoJo, his bistro, in a kitchen with five burners and a single oven. Suarez and Vongerichten continue to be business partners. "He's still there for me every day and I am there for him, like a good marriage. It is trust."

The spartan ambience of JoJo, the paper tablecloths and pared-down menu, was dictated as much by financial constraints as by a vision of simplicity. It was not a propitious moment to open a restaurant, but Vongerichten and Suarez forged ahead and began building an empire.

In March 1997, Vongerichten opened Jean-Georges restaurant in the Trump International Hotel and Tower. Less than three months after opening, Jean-Georges received four stars from Frank Bruni of the *New York Times.*

Vongerichten believes in working as a strong team with members that share his vision and philosophy. They learn from each other. "I want to have an open mind and keep communication open among everyone," says the chef. "We've had the same managers and crews in our restaurants for years. They run their own restaurants. It's all about having the right chefs, the right sous-chefs, and all the other people that it takes to run successful restaurants," he analyzes. "The difficult part is training people to perform to the best of their abilities and to share my food and hospitality philosophies. The chef at JoJo has been with me for eight years and the chef at the New York

Vong and I worked together for fourteen years. We can cook together without even speaking."

About his approach to creating and cooking, Vongerichten says,

"I LOVE TO CREATE, NOT TO REPEAT. FOR FIFTEEN YEARS IN FRANCE, I PREPARED OTHER CHEF'S DISHES. NOW I CHERISH THE OPPORTUNITY TO INVENT NEW FLAVORS AND TASTES, SINCE I HATE TO REPEAT THE SAME OLD THING.

Vongerichten currently runs a multitude of restaurants—eight in New York alone. A partnership with Starwood Hotels gives him the latitude to spread his creativity—and Asian influences—in several new restaurants worldwide. He would open a new restaurant every month, if he had his way.

"He doesn't know how to chill, but he's learning," says Suarez. "His best friend is the kitchen." Vongerichten and his family bought a getaway home in upstate New York in 2007. "As soon as he gets there, he goes right back to his childhood in Alsace—he was a kid with a slingshot, wandering the woods," Suarez says. "It's an adventure for him." For thirty-five years, Vongerichten worked six days a week. Now the family spends most weekends in the country. "It's about time," says Clive Davis, the music mogul and a longtime friend. "The fact that he is balancing his life and participating in the development and growth of his family is remarkable." Vongerichten, a tightly wound, energetic husband and father, has a pond, vegetable garden, guest house, and raises 30,000 bees on four acres.

For all his celebrity, Vongerichten isn't entirely comfortable with frenetic socializing. He loves skiing, hang gliding, and paragliding—anything fast and dangerous—claiming that the best part of any vacation is returning to work. Although he will come out of the kitchen at Jean-Georges to greet an important patron, he's happiest back among his chefs with a pan in hand.

OEUFS *au* CAVIAR

½ cup heavy cream

2 teaspoons fresh lemon juice

2 teaspoons vodka

Salt

4 large eggs

Cayenne pepper

1½ tablespoons butter

2 to 4 teaspoons caviar

1. Whip the cream until it holds stiff peaks, and then season with the lemon juice, vodka, salt, and cayenne. Taste and adjust the seasoning; the flavors should really sing. Whip the cream again until stiff.

2. Remove the tops from the eggshells, pour the eggs into a saucepan or skillet, preferably one with sloping sides, and set the bottoms of the shells in egg cups. Add the butter to the pan and season with salt and cayenne. Turn the heat to medium-high and whisk the egg mixture, stirring almost constantly but not too fast; you do not want it to become foamy.

3. After the butter melts, the mixture will begin to thicken, and then to lump up in small curds; this will take 3 to 8 minutes, depending on the heft of your pan and the heat level. If the mixture begins to stick on the bottom, remove the pan from the heat for a moment, and continue to whisk, then return to the heat.

4. When the eggs become creamy, with small curds all over—not unlike loose oatmeal—they are ready. Do not overcook. Add more salt and cayenne if necessary, and spoon the egg mixture into the eggshells. Use a spoon or a pastry bag to pipe the whipped cream on top of the eggs. Top each with a spoonful of caviar and serve.

SERVES 4

GREEN ASPARAGUS *with* MORELS *and* ASPARAGUS PURÉE

HOLLANDAISE SAUCE

8 large egg yolks

1 tablespoon fresh lemon juice

2 cups butter, diced and soft

Salt

Freshly ground black pepper

Cayenne pepper

MORELS

1 tablespoon butter

1 shallot, diced

8 ounces fresh morel mushrooms (about 2⅓ cups)

1 cup heavy cream

⅓ cup vin jaune (See Note)

ASPARAGUS

1 pound pencil asparagus, unpeeled

Salt

24 stalks jumbo asparagus, peeled

1 tablespoon butter

1. Over a double boiler, cook the egg yolks and lemon juice, whisking until ribbons are formed. Slowly whisk in the butter, and season with salt, pepper, and cayenne. Add water to reach the desired consistency.

2. Warm the butter in a 12-inch sauté pan over medium heat. Sauté the shallots, then add the morels and continue to sauté for 6 to 10 minutes longer. Add the cream and *vin jaune*, bring to a simmer, and simmer for 8 to 10 minutes. Season with salt and pepper. Stir in ½ cup egg mixture. Set aside and keep warm.

3. Trim off and discard the bottom third of the pencil asparagus and thinly slice the spears. Bring a large pot of water to a boil and blanch the asparagus for 10 seconds. Remove with a strainer or slotted spoon and shock in ice water. Reserve the pot of water. In a blender, purée the asparagus until smooth and season with salt.

4. Bring the blanching water back to a boil and cook the jumbo asparagus until done to your taste. Drain the jumbo asparagus and trim the spears to fit onto individual serving plates. In a small saucepan over medium heat, whisk the asparagus purée with the butter until heated through. Arrange the asparagus on the plates and spoon the asparagus purée alongside. Spoon the morels over the asparagus. Serve immediately.

NOTE: *Vin jaune* is a nutty "yellow wine" made in the Jura region of France. It is similar to dry *fino* sherry.

SERVES 4 TO 6

TURBOT *with* CHÂTEAU-CHALON SAUCE

CHÂTEAU-CHALON SAUCE

1½ cups medium-dice carrots

½ cup medium-dice celery

½ cup medium-dice leek whites

½ cup medium-dice onion

2 tablespoons butter

Salt

1 cup white wine

2 quarts chicken stock

2 tablespoons cold butter

3 cups Château-Chalon

1 tablespoon fresh lemon juice

Freshly ground black pepper

FISH

6 turbot fillets (5 ounces each)

Salt

Freshly ground black pepper

2 tablespoons butter, diced

GARNISHES

1 tablespoon butter

1 cup peeled, seeded, and diced tomatoes

1 cup diced zucchini

Fresh lemon juice

To make the Château-Chalon sauce

1. In a large saucepan, sauté the carrots, celery, leeks, and onion in the butter. Sprinkle with salt and sauté until very soft. Add the wine to cover. Reduce by half. Cover with the stock and simmer for 45 minutes. Strain and discard the solids.

2. Return the stock to the saucepan and simmer until reduced by half. Whisk the cold butter into the sauce to add richness and gloss. Finish the sauce with the Château-Chalon and lemon juice and season with salt and pepper. Set aside and keep warm.

To make the fish

1. Preheat the oven to 325°F. Season the turbot with salt and pepper. Scatter the butter in a large ovenproof pan and set the fish on top in a single layer. Bake until the fish is just cooked through, about 6 minutes.

To make the garnish

1. Warm the butter in a medium sauté pan over medium heat. Lightly sauté the tomato and zucchini lightly in the remaining 1 tablespoon butter.

To serve

1. Set 1 piece of fish on each of six warmed plates. Brush each fillet with lemon juice and garnish with the zucchini and tomato. Spoon the sauce around the fish.

SERVES 6

1999

CHARLIE TROTTER

CHARLIE TROTTER LAUGHS A LOT WHEN HE TALKS ABOUT ONCE BEING NAMED THE SECOND MEANEST PERSON IN CHICAGO (MICHAEL JORDAN WON FIRST PLACE AND MAYOR RICHARD DALEY CAME IN THIRD). "It was a tongue-in-cheek thing," Trotter says. "The list was people who are so focused, and so intent on what they do, they want to get it to the next level. Like me. I just want to elevate the game. Or like Mayor Daley, who simply wanted Chicago to be the best city in America. I've had CEOs come into the restaurant and tell me they were upset that they didn't make the top ten." Trotter assured his team at the restaurant that he's aiming for first place.

He even made a cameo appearance in the 1997 film, *My Best Friend's Wedding*, screaming at an assistant, "I will kill your whole family if you don't get this right! I need this perfect!"—in a parody of a stereotypical angry chef. The light side of Trotter may come as a surprise to those outside his inner circle. He's actually friendly and cracks jokes with a W. C. Fields sense of humor. But in the kitchen, Trotter is a tenacious, demanding perfectionist and some consider him America's most formidable chef.

While he may be demanding, Trotter uses reason more than emotion to stimulate total commitment and motivation from staff members, expecting them to be as focused and obsessed as he is. "Any more would almost be perverse. Less so, wouldn't be enough," he says. "That's where you're at a level in your craft, your technique, where you are able to do things spontaneously. That's when we do our finest work—when we're busy, at the most intense. We live for those moments. The difference between degrees of success is a fine line. We want to get to a point when we're worried about competing against ourselves. It takes energy, stamina, experience to push it forward."

Trotter doesn't mind failing in order to learn, and he demands as much from himself as he does from others: "I always say if it didn't take two or three people to replace me when I left, then I've failed." He claims his approach would be the same if he were a gardener or a mechanic. "It's important to try as hard as you can. At the same time, human failings are appealing and beautiful because you learn so much from them. If one knows nothing but success, one can become complacent."

He's occupied with details and observant of surroundings. When he interviews someone, he notices if the person puts the chair back in place. Small things tell him a lot about the person. Trotter believes if a potential employee is detail sensitive, he and his team can do anything with them.

Despite the years of building Charlie Trotter's into an iconic restaurant, Trotter doesn't view the experience as work. "I've never worked in my life," he says. "I'm the luckiest guy in the world. How could you not be psyched to be in a situation where you get to drink great wine every single day? You get to eat amazing food every single day? Who wouldn't like that, right?"

While Trotter has a keen attention to detail, the dishes at his eponymous restaurant are never overplated. Components are placed on the plate spontaneously, playfully, and decoratively. There's always a flowing element to the dish.

An attention to detail was nurtured in Trotter before he began cooking. During high school in Chicago and his first year of college, Trotter's first passion was gymnastics—an activity that no doubt created the balance he's displayed throughout his career.

It wasn't until college, though, that Trotter discovered that cooking was also a sport. "It turned into a competition of who could make the most elaborate five courses." His increasing interest in cooking and restaurants prompted him to take a year's sabbatical from college, working as a waiter and bartender.

He did return to college, graduating with a degree in political science, and then took a three-month trip to Europe to eat and learn. Two experiences there helped form his career. The first, a meal at the late Fernand Point's restaurant, La Pyramide, was magical. Three days later at Girardet in Switzerland, he had another transcendent experience. He says of his epiphany, "All four elements at Girardet were happening in equal measure—the cuisine, the wine, the service, and the overall ambience. It taught me that dining could happen at a spiritual level. When attended to with extraordinary detail, the whole transcends each component beyond the sum of the parts."

On his return to the United States, Trotter went through a lot of jobs in restaurants. He approached each new employment with the plan that he would work at the establishment until he couldn't learn any more. He worked at forty restaurants over a four-year period during his self-imposed training regimen.

Trotter finally felt ready to roll out his own restaurant in 1987 with his father as his partner. "My father spent his youth hustling in pool halls, and started a jazz band called the Trotter Sextet. He played the trumpet and named me for Charlie Parker," explains Trotter. "He worked for a little startup company called IBM, then ultimately opened his own executive recruitment firm with ninety offices around the world. People still come into the restaurant and tell me how grateful they are to my father, that his company helped to change their lives."

Trotter began catering elaborate dinners in people's homes while the restaurant was under construction. "That was the best thing I could have done," he notes, "because when Charlie Trotter's opened its doors, there was already a groundswell of support from the catering customers. We wanted to create an experience so that when someone is leaving, they say: 'We expected a lot and this surpassed all of those expectations.' And that is the same mission today."

Observing Girardet, I learned not to allow flavor to escape. Use pristine products. Visually, you have to make love to food while you cook. If you can embrace that approach to things, then you can coax something to another level, you can really make it spectacular."

Some chefs devise signature dishes that become fixtures on their menus; people come to that restaurant to experience that dish. Then there are chefs like Girardet or David Bouley (the James Beard Foundation's Outstanding Chef, 2000), who have no signature dish. Their menus are more fluid, not fixed, always changing. One day a set of ingredients is prepared. The next day the chefs might have the same ingredients, but do something else with them, emphasizing a different flavor. A year later with the same ingredients, it could be reinterpreted altogether.

When Trotter thinks of John Coltrane, or of Miles Davis, he remembers that they never played a song the same way twice. "They might speed up the tempo, Coltrane would switch to a different sax, or Miles would mute his horn—the song would keep evolving and changing. This is more the style of Frédy Girardet. To cook like that, one must know combinations; one must have a true knowledge of food to be in the moment," Trotter says. "Alfred Portale (the James Beard Foundation Outstanding Chef, 2006) once said, 'Any young cook with a couple of squeeze bottles can be a dangerous character.' Similarly, you could have a young musician who is in a famous punk band, but could he play jazz music? He would not have enough knowledge of the fundamental elements of music."

YOU NEED TO MAKE A DIFFERENCE WITH WHAT YOU DO IN LIFE. THAT'S FROM A PROFESSIONAL STANDPOINT, AN AESTHETIC STANDPOINT, AND HOPEFULLY FROM A PHILANTHROPIC STANDPOINT, AND IF YOU CAN WALK AWAY WITH THAT AS A TEAM MEMBER THEN YOU'VE LEARNED A LOT."

He's concerned about inspiring people to think, especially people who have worked for him. Trotter is also personally involved with his philanthropic Charlie Trotter Culinary Education Foundation and other causes. He was awarded the Humanitarian of the Year award in 2005 by the International Association of Culinary Professionals. He invites groups of public high school students into his restaurant as part of his Excellence in Action Program three times per week: They eat a meal and are told how the food was prepared and the motivations of those preparing it, helping the students get in touch with their passions. "I do a lot because I want to and I'm in a position to do a lot," Trotter says. "But I think anyone who is drawn to this world of food, wine, and service—it's kind of in your nature to want to do things for people. You're doing one of the most intimate things you can for another person in feeding them."

GREEN BELGIUM WHITE ASPARAGUS *with* BLACKBERRIES

ASPARAGUS

16 stalks white asparagus (about 1 pound)

Squirt fresh lemon juice

2 tablespoons olive oil

2 tablespoons chopped fresh chervil and fresh parley, combined

1 tablespoon blackberry powder

YOGURT

1 cup organic plain yogurt

1 tablespoon agave syrup

1 teaspoon smoked sea salt

MARINATED BLACKBERRIES

1 tablespoon aged balsamic vinegar

1 tablespoon olive oil

3 cups organic blackberries

BLACKBERRY PURÉE

2 cups organic blackberries

3 tablespoons balsamic vinegar

2 tablespoons olive oil

Salt

GREENS

1 handful red ribbon sorrel (about 1 ounce)

1 handful nasturtium flowers (about 1 ounce)

1 handful chervil (about 1 ounce)

To make the asparagus

1. Trim asparagus, removing all tough fibers, reserving trimmings and spears separately. In a medium saucepan over high heat, bring 1 quart water and the trimmings to a boil. Cover and reduce heat; simmer for 20 minutes. Drain, reserving the stock.

2. In an upright steamer, pour in enough asparagus stock to cover the bottom of the pot by 1 to 2 inches. Add the asparagus spears, lemon juice, and olive oil. Bring to a simmer, cover, and steam for 10 minutes, or until the spears are soft. Remove the spears and keep warm or let cool completely.

3. Prepare a medium fire in a grill. Grill the asparagus until lightly browned on all sides, about 3 minutes.

4. Toss half of the asparagus spears with the chopped chervil and parsley. Toss the other half with the blackberry powder.

CONTINUED

To make the yogurt

1. In a bowl, combine the yogurt, agave syrup, and smoked salt.

To marinate the blackberries

1. In a medium bowl, whisk together the vinegar and oil to make a vinaigrette. Add the black-berries and marinate for a minimum of 5 minutes or up to 8 minutes. Drain the berries and reserve the vinaigrette.

To make the blackberry purée

1. Combine the blackberries, balsamic vinegar, and olive oil in a blender and purée until smooth. Season with salt.

To make the greens

1. In a large bowl, combine the sorrel, nasturtium, and chervil.

To serve

1. Drizzle each plate with some of the blackberry purée. With a mixer, whip the yogurt until soft peaks form. Place a portion of the marinated berries on each plate. Top the berries with about 1 tablespoon of the yogurt. To each plate, add 2 each of the herbed asparagus spears and the asparagus spears tossed with blackberry powder. Toss the greens with the reserved vinaigrette and divide evenly among the plates.

SERVES 4

SQUAB BREAST *with* FRENCH BREAKFAST RADISH CONFIT, BLACK SESAME PURÉE, *and* ANNATTO GASTRIQUE

SESAME SEED TUILES

1 cup unsalted butter

1 cup sugar

2/3 cup glucose

3 3/4 cups black sesame seeds

2/3 cup milk

RADISH CONFIT

1 bunch French breakfast radishes with greens

2 tablespoons duck fat

1 tablespoon annatto seeds

ANNATTO GASTRIQUE

1 cup sugar

1/4 cup annatto seeds

1 tablespoon freshly grated ginger

1 teaspoon lemongrass paste

1/4 cup sherry vinegar

BLACK SESAME PURÉE

2 tablespoons olive oil

3 Honeycrisp apples, peeled and chopped

2 shallots, minced

1 garlic clove, minced

1/2 cup black sesame seeds

2 cups vegetable stock

CHICKEN LIVER PURÉE

2 tablespoons olive oil

1 pound chicken livers

1 cup peeled and chopped Granny Smith apples

1 onion, diced

2 garlic cloves, minced

1/4 cup white wine

1 tablespoon chopped fresh thyme

Salt

Freshly ground black pepper

SQUAB

1 whole squab (about 1 1/2 pounds)

1 tablespoon duck fat

1 tablespoon minced shallot

Microgreens, for garnish

To make the sesame seed tuiles

1. Preheat the oven to 375°F. Melt the butter, sugar, and glucose in a medium saucepan over medium heat, but do not let the mixture boil. Add the sesame seeds and milk. Spread the batter evenly into 3-inch circles spaced 1 inch apart on a baking sheet lined with a silicone baking mat. Bake for 10 to 15 minutes. Shape the warm tuiles and leave them to cool.

To make the radish confit

1. Scrub the radishes and remove the radish greens, reserving 1/2 cup. Sous vide the radishes in the duck fat and the annatto at 185°F for 2 hours. (If the sous vide method is not available, slice the radishes and put them in a saucepan. Sprinkle with the annatto seeds and cover with

CONTINUED

the duck fat. Cook uncovered over the lowest heat, keeping the temperature at about 200°F, for 2 hours. Using a slotted spoon, remove the radishes and place them in a crock. Increase the heat to medium-high and cook the fat until it stops sputtering, 5 to 10 minutes. Drain through a fine sieve, discarding the solids. Pour the fat into the crock, completely covering the radishes.) Refrigerate.

To make the annatto gastrique

1. Add the sugar to a saucepan over medium-low heat. When the sugar begins to caramelize, add the annatto seeds and continue to cook, stirring continuously, until brown, 6 to 7 minutes. Add the ginger and lemongrass and cook for 2 minutes. Deglaze with the vinegar. Simmer the mixture until reduced by half and strain, reserving the liquid.

To make the sesame purée

1. Warm the oil in a medium skillet or sauté pan over high heat. Add the apples, shallots, and garlic and sauté until the mixture is soft, about 10 minutes. Add the black sesame seeds and sauté until fragrant. Add the stock and simmer for 6 minutes. Purée the mixture in a high-speed blender. Strain through a *chinois*. Reserve.

To make the chicken liver purée

1. Warm the oil in a large skillet or sauté pan over high heat. Add the chicken livers and sear until golden brown. Remove the livers and set aside. Add the apples, onion, and garlic to the skillet and sauté over medium heat until softened and translucent, about 4 minutes. Transfer the mixture to a high-speed blender. Deglaze the skillet with the wine and stir in the thyme. Add the seared livers and the wine to the blender and purée until the mixture is smooth. Season with salt and pepper. Reserve warm.

To make the squab

1. Preheat the oven to 350°F. Remove the legs of the squab and reserve for another use. Keep the wings attached to the breast. Season the squab with salt and pepper. In a medium skillet or sauté pan over high heat, sear the squab on all sides. Remove the squab with a slotted spoon and put it in a roasting pan. Roast for 10 minutes, to finish cooking.

2. Remove the squab and let it rest for about 8 minutes while making the radish greens. In a skillet, warm the duck fat and sauté the reserved radish greens. Add the shallot, the radish confit, and the annatto gastrique. Sauté until the greens are slightly wilted, 1 to 2 minutes. Place the greens in the center of two serving plates.

3. Slice the squab and arrange it on the greens. Coat it with jus from the roasting pan. Drizzle black sesame purée and chicken liver purée over each plate, garnish with a tuile, and serve.

SERVES 2

2000

DAVID BOULEY

CHAPTER *eleven*

AS THE *ENFANT TERRIBLE* OF THE 1970S AND 1980S CULI-NARY FRONT LINE, DAVID BOULEY TRAINED IN FRANCE. Like many others, he worked for nothing (or, almost nothing but food) and *staged* with nouvelle cuisine masters, had his butt kicked, became a target for flying utensils, and was yelled at in languages not his own.

Making a fair trade, he came home with the self-confidence, discipline, knowledge, and techniques to begin transforming modern American cuisine. Armed with energy and little patience, he now had the chops to break tradition and drive a stake through old-school perceptions of fine dining. Bouley was ready for the hard-scrabble climb to become what Charlie Trotter, the 1999 James Beard Foundation Outstanding Chef, called "the most influential chef in the United States."

"A handsome young man came almost every day to my pastry shop in Santa Fe," reminisces Michel Richard, now the renowned chef of Citronelle in Washington, D.C., and the 2007 James Beard Foundation Outstanding Chef. "His dream was to become a chef. When he wanted to go to France, I helped him find a job. Look at the results—he has become one of the top chefs of this country." Richard is understandably proud, and Bouley is not the only chef he's sponsored.

Bouley is embarrassed when reminded that he was named one of *People* magazine's "50 Most Beautiful People" in 1994. But as attractive as he is, his culinary style and talent supersede all else.

Bouley was born and raised near Storrs, Connecticut. The second of nine children, he was influenced by farm life and his heritage as the grandson of French émigrés. "My roots are definitely French," he says. "I'm a cook of ingredients. I was raised on a farm."

Uncertain about a career as a chef, he began working in restaurants simply because he needed the job, and he spent time in restaurants in Santa Fe, New Mexico, and Cape Cod, Massachusetts. After studying business at the Sorbonne, in Paris, though, he worked in restaurants in France and Switzerland.

In France, Bouley apprenticed, worked, and *staged* with some of Europe's most acclaimed chefs, including Roger Vergé, Paul Bocuse, Joël Robuchon, Gaston Lenôtre, and Frédy Girardet. Returning to the United States in 1980, he sharpened his skills in Manhattan's leading restaurants of the time—Le Cirque, Le Périgord, and La Côte Basque—as well as working as sous-chef at Roger Vergé's restaurant in San Francisco.

Teaming with Drew Nieporent, who he met in San Francisco, Bouley opened Montrachet in New York City in 1985. Bouley, seeking innovation, offered the first American *dégustation* menu—miniscule servings of a few exquisite bites designed, then refined, for flavor, texture, and anticipation. "We stimulate the palate, keeping the momentum moving all the way through the experience," explains Bouley.

Two years later, he took another path, opening Bouley. He established his signature style there: superior quality and tiny courses, with several different offerings inspired by an individual guest, the season, the mood, or the moment.

His new restaurant was immediately a premiere dining experience, celebrity-studded, and sparkling with four-star reviews. Glitterati swooned. Accolades, rankings, and multiple awards quickly followed. From 1991 until it closed in 1996, Bouley was voted the most popular restaurant in New York by the Zagat Survey and received an unparalleled food rating of 29 out of 30 in the last three years. The *New York Times* restaurant critic, Bryan Miller, gave Bouley four stars, writing, "David Bouley's rabid zeal for fresh regional ingredients, his cerebral approach to textures and flavors, and his obvious delight in wowing customers make this one of the most exciting restaurants in New York City."

Always a pioneer, Bouley worked with universities and farmers to grow vegetables for and fostered the development of such artisanal produce as fingerling potatoes. His style of nutritious food balanced with beauty became paramount for him. "It's a French approach to cooking that means a strong understanding of the history and the repertoire. It's an interrelationship of products and a good understanding of technique, then employing all of them at the same time," he explains.

He uses a minimum of cream and butter, relying instead on an almost worshipful approach to ingredients for depth and richness. He speaks with great feeling of food that goes straight "to your body and to your soul. Clean, pure food—as a chef, you can't go beyond that. When you know that, and when you cook like that, is when you develop your own style. Nature can give you something so memorable." Bouley's extraordinary flavors are clear and exquisitely balanced. His seasoning is deft with complex creations in a classical simplicity.

Yet Bouley has always been provocative, following his own path, rather than one prescribed for a celebrity chef. What chef would successfully open for a time, then close dynamic restaurants once they were firmly established? One who is always impatient, exploring cuisines and ambiance, quite simply invigorated by challenges. One who proves his point, curiosity satisfied, or as the market changes, always moving ahead. Everything is built around his vision, powered by a restless intellect and persistence.

Bouley doesn't see obstacles. Focused and controlled, he melds them into opportunities. He listens carefully, selectively, and becomes totally absorbed. Then, intrigued, emboldened by a concept, he breaks into action. "I need to have spontaneity and I work at the last minute," Bouley confesses. "If I think too far ahead, I dilute myself." He's fast, and relatively fearless both in and out of the kitchen. He proved that racing motorcycles for Ducati in the 1960s, and later blasting around Manhattan on a Harley.

Central casting could have sent him onto a movie set as an eccentric chef. Protégés adore him and appreciate his quirks. Cooks who are puzzled by it all don't make the cut. Bouley conceptualizes, cooks with jubilant abandon, and at the same time is a masterful technician. To work with Bouley is to be flexible, and most of all, intuitive, and in tune with him. At various times during service, he'll change a recipe, or even change the menu. His spontaneity keeps his cooks excited and vigilant. "If they get complacent and into a routine groove, the food tastes bland. If the cook is alert, on edge, it is reflected in the food."

Bouley's imagination is sparked in an extreme environment. If the pressure isn't there, he cranks it up to another level. It stimulates the creativity he uses to refine everything when he relaxes enough to get into a mindset where most people stress or freeze. His technique is instinctive from decades of execution, and daring. "Why not?" he asks. "Why not now?" Never, "How?"

The 2009 James Beard Foundation Outstanding Chef Dan Barber described the inner workings of the Bouley kitchen as "controlled chaos." The atmosphere was intense. It was also, as Barber remembers, confusing. "Around him, there is an orbit of madness."

Certainly nothing about him is static. Since the original Bouley opened in 1987, the resilient chef has developed and tested several concepts: Danube, an Austrian restaurant; then Secession, his New York bistro in the old Danube space; and the newest experiment, Brushstroke, a Japanese notion on West Broadway. Since the destruction of September 11th in lower Manhattan in 2001, Bouley Bakery, part of the original restaurant group in TriBeCa, has moved to new quarters and been reimagined as a smaller, finer concept. His Upstairs restaurant has morphed into a more casual dining spot for baked goods and takeout. His aim is now more targeted, and objectives precise. Transformation is important to him.

Bouley restaurant is his flagship, though, and the keystone of his TriBeCa epicurean empire. The original closed in 1996; the current incarnation opened in 2008.

The dramatic vaulted arches in the newest Bouley are a stunning design built in tandem with his contractor brother, Martin. They discussed the possibilities, built it, ripped it out, and started over, doing it again and again until they were satisfied. That was the same aesthetic and willingness to revise that is echoed in his approach to his menus.

The front doors, made of walnut, were salvaged from a sixteenth-century abbey in Provence, France. A master craftsman restored the doors and six eighteenth-century wooden beams across the lounge area ceiling. Through another master artisan, Bouley secured twenty tons of stone for the fireplace, walls, and staircases from a long-closed quarry in France used to build Versailles. Bouley's restaurant was the only project outside France to receive the stone. The meticulously cut stones were carefully arranged according to their color, shape, and texture to replicate intricate, historical patterns. The vestibule is lined with narrow shelves of fresh apples, producing an orchard of fragrance, a hint of surprises ahead.

Large Impressionist-style paintings, commissioned from artist Claude Chevally, grace the dining room. A massive limestone fireplace warms the interior, with tapered candles reflecting off vaulted gold-leafed ceilings and silvered walls. The room shimmers with lush fabrics, saturated colors, and lustrous glazed surfaces.

By contrast, his test kitchen research facility, with its state-of-the-art equipment, provides ongoing stimulation and education for Bouley and his staff. On occasion, food enthusiasts are invited to spend time learning the alchemy in his private sanctum. Bouley collects talent in many fields, bringing them together for collaboration. He invites other chefs, cheesemakers, vintners, and food experts from around the world for freewheeling brainstorming sessions of technique, new ingredients, and trends. A huge slate wall acts as a blackboard for doodling ideas. Oversized video screens project the work in progress, and an adjacent library contains fine culinary resources.

Bouley thrives on executing an idea. It could be a thoughtful process or a whimsical one. His immaculate kitchen is calibrated to his pace. Cooks work at a custom-made Molteni, the Ferrari of gas stoves. He communicates at times without words, directing the brigade with a searing glare, an arched eyebrow, or an impatient gesture.

One now-famous chef chuckles as he recalls his first day in the kitchen when Bouley instructed him to talk to a fish. It was the chef's metaphor to explain that every fish, like every person, is different. A cook must be sensitive to nuance and communication is essential, extending to all foods. He insists that cooks look at, and consider, each product. He tries to learn from every situation. Bouley says,

"IT'S ABOUT REACHING A POINT OF TAKING YOUR CLASSICAL CULINARY INFLUENCES AND DEVELOPING A VOICE OF YOUR OWN. IT IS ABOUT UNDERSTANDING HOW TO ENHANCE THE NATURAL BEAUTY OF A FRUIT OR A PIECE OF FISH, RATHER THAN OBSCURING IT WITH INAPPROPRIATE HERBS AND SPICES."

The kitchen has always dictated his personal life, so it's fitting that Bouley met his wife on the day that Danube closed. Nicole Bartelme, a Rhode Island School of Design graduate, runs the philanthropic organization TriBeCa Native, founded the TriBeCa Film Festival, and has a hand in Bouley's restaurant projects. "David and I have very similar tastes, so we work very well together," says the artist and photographer.

"Restaurants start when the guests sit down at the tables, and cooking can only be considered an art once the customer has finished the last bite," Bouley believes, already thinking ahead to his next creation.

SEA URCHIN TERRINE *with* CRÉME FRAÎCHE, OESTRA CAVIAR, *and* FRESH *KINOME*

3 sheets gelatin

3 cups Dashi (page 127)

2½ tablespoons soy sauce

1 tablespoon mirin

1 tablespoon sake

6 ounces fresh shelled sea urchin

1 cup crème fraîche

1 teaspoon yuzu juice

1 teaspoon diced shallots

1 teaspoon fresh lime juice

1 bunch chives

Salt

Freshly ground black pepper

4 fresh *kinome* (prickly ash leaves)

2 ounces osetra caviar

1. Soften the gelatin sheets in cold water to cover, about 15 minutes.

2. To a medium saucepan over low heat, add the dashi, soy sauce, mirin, and sake.

3. Remove the gelatin and squeeze out excess water. Add it to the dashi mixture and stir until the gelatin has melted. Pour the mixture into 9-by-5-inch terrine mold. Let it stand at room temperature until almost set.

4. Arrange the sea urchin on the surface of the gelatin in the terrine. Refrigerate until firm.

5. In a bowl, whisk together the crème fraîche, yuzu, shallots, and lime juice. Season with salt and pepper.

6. Put the chives in a blender or food processor and purée. With the motor running, add the oil to the blender in a stream. Continue to purée until smooth. Season with salt and pepper.

To assemble

1. Spoon the yuzu crème fraîche onto each serving plate. Unmold and cut the terrine into 1-inch-thick slices and place 1 slice on each plate. Garnish with chive oil, *kinome*, and caviar and serve.

NOTE: Chive oil is another wonderful—and colorful—garnish for this dish. To make chive oil, purée 1 cup of coarsely chopped fresh chives in a blender or food processor. With the machine running, stream in 3/4 cup soybean or grapeseed oil and process until the mixture is smooth. Season the oil with salt and pepper to taste. Drizzle the oil over the plated terrine slices.

SERVES 6

PORCINI FLAN *with* DUNGENESS CRAB *and* BLACK TRUFFLE DASHI

DASHI SAUCE

2 tablespoons kudzu powder

1 cup Dashi (page 127)

1 teaspoon mirin

1 tablespoon fresh ginger juice (squeezed from grated fresh ginger)

2 tablespoons light soy sauce

2 to 4 ounces jumbo lump crabmeat, plus extra for garnish

4 to 6 ounces black truffle pâté

MUSHROOM PURÉE

1½ to 2 tablespoons olive oil

1 pound porcini or royal trumpet mushrooms, thinly sliced

Salt

Freshly ground black pepper

FLAN

3 small brown eggs

1 cup Dashi (page 127)

6 fresh *kinome* (prickly ash leaves)

To make the dashi sauce

1. In a small bowl, stir the kudzu into 1 ounce of cold water until smooth. In a small saucepan, heat the dashi until warm and add the mirin. Add the kudzu mixture and stir until the mixture thickens. Add the ginger juice and soy sauce.

2. Add the crabmeat to a bowl and add dashi mixture to cover. In a second bowl, combine the remaining dashi mixture with the pâté. Cover and keep warm.

To make the mushroom purée

1. In a large sauté pan, warm the olive oil and cook the mushrooms until tender. Purée the mushrooms in a food processor and season with salt and pepper.

To make the flan

1. Preheat the oven to 325°F. Whisk the eggs, then pour in the dashi and blend. Pass the mixture through a strainer, then divide it among six 4-ounce ramekins. Set the ramekins in a roasting pan or large baking dish and add hot water to the pan to come about halfway up the sides of the ramekins. Cover the pan and bake until the tip of a knife inserted into the center of the flans comes out clean, 8 to 10 minutes.

To serve

1. Spread 2 tablespoons of the mushroom purée on each cooked flan. Add a 1-inch-thick layer of the dashi-crabmeat mixture on top of each flan and finish with a ¼-inch-thick layer of the dashi-pâté mixture. Garnish with additional crabmeat and the *kinome*. Serve warm.

NOTE: If you do not eat crab, the recipe works very well with asparagus or corn instead.

SERVES 6

DASHI

1 quart cold water, plus extra as needed (use Volvic bottled water for best results)

1 ounce giant kelp (*kombu*)

1 ounce dried bonito flakes (*hana-katsuo*)

1. Fill a medium pot with the water and put in the kelp. Bring to just below a boil, about 10 minutes. Remove the *kombu* before the water boils to avoid a strong odor. Test by inserting your thumbnail into the fleshiest part. If the flesh is tough, return the *kombu* to the pot for 1 or 2 minutes. If necessary to prevent boiling, add ¼ cup cold water. When the flesh is soft, remove the *kombu* and discard.

2. Bring the liquid to a boil. Add ¼ cup cold water to bring the temperature down quickly and immediately add the bonito flakes. Bring to a boil again and immediately remove from the heat to avoid bitterness. Allow the flakes to settle, about 30 to 60 seconds. Skim foam. Filter the stock through a cheesecloth-lined sieve, reserving the bonito and kelp to make a secondary dashi, if desired.

MAKES 1 QUART

2001

PATRICK O'CONNELL

CHAPTER *twelve*

IT'S NOT SURPRISING THAT PATRICK O'CONNELL'S COLLEGE MAJOR WAS DRAMA. FANS HAVE COME TO THINK OF HIM AS A THEATRICAL PRODUCER DISGUISED AS A SELF-TAUGHT CHEF, RESTAURATEUR, AND INNKEEPER. The late winemaker Robert Mondavi dubbed him the "pope of American cuisine." In the *International Herald Tribune*, Patricia Wells described him as "a rare chef with a sense of near-perfect taste, like a musician with perfect pitch."

In the tiny historic town of Washington, Virginia, in the foothills of the Blue Ridge Mountains, O'Connell has created his own joyous theater in the round, as chef/proprietor of The Inn at Little Washington. O'Connell's idyllic set includes the kitchen, front and center, whereas most culinary crews work backstage. At The Inn, the cooks are outfitted in black jackets paired with O'Connell's signature dalmatian-spot chef's pants. He's the only one wearing a white jacket, though he's easy to notice because of his in-charge presence. His kitchen is dressed up in chandeliers, paintings, objets d'art, hand-painted Portuguese tiles, and two guest tables that act as ringside seats. An immense brass-trimmed Vulcan range with a brass and copper hood centers it all.

For a man who began a catering business in the 1970s with a wood-burning stove and a cheap electric frying pan, the custom-built French range is a monumental reminder of his success. It's the *pièce de résistance* in a kitchen designed to be the restaurant's heart—and its stage.

O'Connell draws inspiration from unlikely sources. Early on, he envisioned life as a film, so in his imagination he creates cohesive experiences, with a beginning, middle, and end. His showplace kitchen and entertaining concepts were influenced by two things: The dairy room at Windsor Castle and the movie *The Cook, the Thief, His Wife, and Her Lover*, by Peter Greenaway.

In the Greenaway film, the kitchen was an otherworldly kind of heavenly environment. "They had a eunuch dishwasher singing in almost a falsetto. The space was both transporting and inspiring, with an element of the kitchen being a separate place," says O'Connell. "We like to bring the kitchen into the experience here. It's unique—it's both like being in a private home and also going to the opera."

The charm and serenity of the town of Washington and the rolling Virginia countryside reflect O'Connell's goal of offering visitors a healing, restorative escape—the preparation and presentation of food being but one element of the overall experience. He knows that even a small flaw can shatter an illusion, and he obsesses over producing a cocooned fantasy for guests.

"For me, food is pretty simple," he says. "But it's only one element of transporting people.

I READ RECENTLY THAT FOOD ACTUALLY TASTES BETTER AND IS MORE ENJOYABLE IN A SITUATION OF TOTAL RELAXATION, CALM, AND TRANQUILITY. I ALWAYS FEEL THAT IS THE KEY, PUTTING PEOPLE IN THAT EXACT FRAME OF MIND TO FULLY APPRECIATE IT. AND I THINK THAT THAT'S THE GREATER CHALLENGE THAN JUST PRODUCING OUTSTANDING FOOD."

"Patrick has been an amazing leader," chef Daniel Boulud once said. Boulud first met O'Connell when Boulud arrived in Washington, D.C., as a private chef in 1980. "He was one of the first to create a standard here. He's always given more than just good cooking. He makes people feel special."

Although O'Connell's culinary concepts are what he calls "simple," it would probably be more accurate to say that his instincts are keen, giving his guests the feeling of utter delight.

"For years people would ask, 'What kind of food do you serve in your restaurant?' and it drove me crazy because they were looking for a one- or two-word handle. They were able to bring all their preconceptions or prejudices into the picture so I realized that it was fraught with a kind of hex no matter what you said, nothing worked. If you said 'American' it either meant nothing, or meatloaf and fried chicken," he says. "I finally found three words that satisfied me, that illustrated the point, and they are 'refined American cuisine.'"

By taking popular childhood dishes and making them contemporary, O'Connell creates a culinary link between past and future. His approach to cooking reflects a belief in the cuisine of today—healthy, eclectic, imaginative, unrestricted by ethnic boundaries, and ever evolving, while paying homage to classical French foundations.

"Such an approach also allows us to be playful, and that's something that was never permitted before, particularly by European culinary culture. It had to be taken very seriously," he says. "I think humor is a very powerful tool, and you can bring the dishes forward with a twist. I think it's so easy to do the predictable, but what I like to do is master the expected and then introduce a note of startling unexpectedness."

O'Connell realized after spending time in Europe that American culture had finally reached a crossroads where there were actually two cuisines—home cooking and haute cuisine. "My frustration always was that we were programmed to believe that the French had the right to revere their childhood food memories of sausage from Lyon or ham from Bayonne and we felt that we should ridicule our own. I think all of our personal food memories are just as legitimate and viable and they should be treasured and revered."

So just how does O'Connell revere the childhood foods of Americans? He explains the dichotomy of his creations: "What I've been attempting to do for all these years is take my flavor memories, bring them forward, and turn them into something that could be laid side-by-side with the greatest dishes from the greatest restaurants in Europe. So they could be in harmony and be at one with them. The challenge for American chefs is to continue to do that and not turn our backs on mom's pineapple upside-down cake—all the tastes that were a part of our childhoods that we can use to build upon."

O'Connell relishes entertaining as an occasion for personal flourishes that bring together food, ambiance, and performance. When he produces an event, he orchestrates and choreographs all the details. He holds dress rehearsals with the kitchen and service staff. The dishes are prepared and served as practice so that glitches can be worked out and refinements made to heighten the experience for the guests. "I recommend that home cooks do this a week before having a party. It may seem excessive, but it gets rid of the stress of wondering what will work and what won't," he says. "A host or hostess who's having fifty people over knows about planning," he says. "You still worry how it's all going to come together." The key is mastery, and mastery gives the cook confidence, he believes. "I suggest choosing a three-course menu. Make it once a week on a Sunday afternoon. After repetition, that menu can be put together quickly," says O'Connell. "It will be refined and honed until no one can do it better. And the cook is truly a master of that and it's their entertaining menu. Then, they can branch off, and can add things, but it gives them an incredible foundation. It is what I did."

O'Connell grew up in Washington, D.C., and made visits to the Virginia countryside with his family. After finishing college, he acted on the advice of a family friend who suggested that he buy some property before embarking on his European travels so he would have something to which he could return. That property was a tiny, unheated mountain shack where it all began. O'Connell came home, moved in, and taught himself to cook and bake on his wood-burning stove.

In the 1970s, O'Connell and a former partner began catering for well-to-do families in the Shenandoah Valley. But drawing on his experiences abroad, O'Connell developed a vision of creating a luxurious European-style country inn that would serve refined American cuisine in a unique setting. When word got around town that O'Connell planned to open a restaurant, no one knew what to expect. The general attitude was that it was folly. If you had any sense or business acumen, why would you choose the middle of nowhere as a location? Nonetheless, O'Connell's aim was high and sure when he began the seven-year process required to open the restaurant. "The constant refrain was 'Who's coming?'" remembers O'Connell. "And I heard it over and over again. I just didn't think about who was coming, I just thought people would come."

When The Inn at Little Washington opened in 1978, it was housed in a one-time garage—the rent was $200 a month. "The stakes then were a little different than they are now," O'Connell acknowledges. "The challenge was keeping hot food hot and cold food cold. And if you did that and were nice to people, they were usually ever so grateful. So astonishing them then and astonishing them now is two totally different challenges."

Guests streamed in and they continue to do so. First ladies, Supreme Court justices, celebrities, and culinary sophisticates make the journey to The Inn for the grace, the ambiance, and the food. "People who come here—and they come here, no question—they get off the main road from the city, and the countryside is a culture shock, but in a charming, delightful sort of way," he says. "It actually accentuates the distance between their world and this world. So it's more fun to kind of create an oasis and fantasy and ecstasy in these surroundings."

From the very beginning, decades before the term "locavore" was coined, O'Connell forged alliances with local growers and artisans. He cultivated relationships with neighbors—many with strong connections to the land and a heritage of self-sufficiency—who could supply him with the products he needed. These were socially responsible actions, but also necessary ones—he insisted on using only the finest, freshest foods, but back then, the only thing delivered was milk, and restaurant suppliers wouldn't drive out to such a remote little town.

Shortly after the restaurant's opening, a Washington, D.C., newspaper declared it the best restaurant in a 150-mile radius. "That was frightening," admits O'Connell. "Oddly enough, the reviewer in his opening line said, 'Every once in a while a restaurant comes along that's so good you worry,' and I think he could imagine the public's reaction when he gave it a rave review. So for ten years, I didn't really feel like I had come up for air. I just cooked as fast as I could."

There's been a lot of cooking in O'Connell's kitchen since then, and there's much more to come. How can someone emulate this kind of personal and professional fulfillment?

"I absorbed everything on the job," he emphasizes. "But having the great opportunity early on to visit some of the best restaurants in the world and be able to feel it and work toward replicating that feeling was enormously useful." O'Connell continues quarterly visits to Europe, opportunities for further exposure, as American Culinary Ambassador for the prestigious Relais & Châteaux, an organization of the world's finest restaurants and hotels. He's currently president of the United States chapter.

"Our industry has just grown and accelerated to the point where it's on an incredible fast track, and, in spite of the economy, people are working incredibly hard and creatively. And there's newness everywhere," he observes. "We're probably working harder now than we've ever worked and in a more focused way, to continue to refine every aspect. It's not getting easier."

With The Inn at Little Washington, O'Connell never anticipated an easy path, but his business adventures wound up embracing a town and today his pioneering efforts are legendary. The town was just about bankrupt when The Inn opened. Now, finances are healthy, and the majority of the town's budget is based on local meals and lodging tax generated by The Inn. Staffed with 108 employees, The Inn is also a major employer. On a busy evening, the restaurant may serve 200 guests, more than the town's population of 183 residents.

O'Connell continues his community involvement, currently serving as Chairman of the Architectural Review Board for the town council. He plans to further renovate and add to The Inn. Systematically acquiring and restoring his properties, he has made an addition of nearly twenty-five acres of meadow with views of the Blue Ridge Mountains. He hopes to eventually add orchards and livestock to provide food for the restaurant.

It's no exaggeration to say that O'Connell put the town of Washington, Virginia, on the culinary map.

CARPACCIO *of* HERB-CRUSTED BABY LAMB *with* CAESAR SALAD ICE CREAM

PESTO

2 cups packed fresh basil

¼ cup pine nuts

¼ cup fresh parsley

2 garlic cloves

⅔ cup extra-virgin olive oil

½ cup freshly grated Parmigiano-Reggiano

Fresh lemon juice

Sugar

Kosher salt

Freshly ground black pepper

CROUTONS

2 cups grapeseed oil

1 garlic clove

1 sprig fresh rosemary

6 baguette slices, cut into 1-inch cubes (about 2 cups)

LAMB CARPACCIO

1 to 1½ pounds lamb loin

½ cup dried oregano

½ cup dried thyme

½ cup dried basil

½ cup dried tarragon

Grapeseed oil, for searing

CAESAR DRESSING

1 large egg yolk

6 tablespoons red wine vinegar

1 tablespoon fresh lemon juice

2 teaspoons Dijon mustard

1½ teaspoons Worcestershire sauce

1 ounce Parmigiano-Reggiano, grated

1½ garlic cloves, minced

1 anchovy fillet, minced

Pinch of cayenne pepper

⅓ cup olive oil

¼ cup salad oil

CAESAR SALAD ICE CREAM

7 large egg yolks

⅓ cup sugar

4⅓ cups whole milk

¾ cup powdered milk

1⅓ cups freshly grated Parmigiano-Reggiano

4 anchovy fillets, minced

2 tablespoons minced garlic

Worcestershire sauce, for seasoning

Dijon mustard, for seasoning

GARNISHES

Red pearl onions, thinly sliced into rounds

Capers

Chives, finely chopped

Baby arugula

4 to 6 hearts of romaine leaves

Parmigiano-Reggiano, grated

CONTINUED

To make the pesto

1. In a blender or food processor, combine the basil, pine nuts, parsley, and garlic. Purée until smooth. Add the oil in a thin stream. Add the Parmigiano-Reggiano. Press through a fine-mesh strainer, then season with the lemon juice, sugar, salt, and pepper. Reserve, chilled.

To make the croutons

1. In a heavy 1-quart saucepan over high heat, warm the grapeseed oil. Add the garlic to infuse the oil. When the garlic is brown, remove and discard. Fry the rosemary sprig for 30 to 45 seconds, remove, and discard. Fry the croutons for 2 to 3 minutes, or until golden. Remove the croutons, drain on towels, and season with salt. Reserve warm.

To make the lamb

1. Remove all visible sinew and fat from the lamb loin. Season with salt and pepper. Let rest for 15 minutes. In a small bowl, combine the herbs. Coat the loin with the herb mixture. To a large heavy-bottomed skillet over high heat, add the grapeseed oil to a depth of $1/4$ inch. Heat the oil and evenly sear the lamb. Place it on a cooling rack. Once cooled, roll the loin tightly in plastic wrap to form a sausage shape. Freeze until ready to slice.

To make the dressing

1. Combine the yolk, vinegar, lemon juice, mustard, Worcestershire sauce, Parmigiano-Reggiano, garlic, anchovies, and cayenne in a food processor or blender. With the motor running, add the oils in a thin stream to until desired thickness is reached. Season with salt and pepper. Reserve, chilled.

To make the ice cream

1. In a large bowl, whisk together the yolks and sugar. In a large heavy saucepan over high heat, bring the milk, powdered milk, Parmigiano-Reggiano, anchovies, and garlic to a boil. Add the mixture to the yolks, stirring constantly. Return the mixture to the saucepan and cook over low heat, stirring until thick enough to coat the back of a spoon. Remove from the heat and let cool. Season to taste with Worcestershire sauce, mustard, salt, and pepper.

2. Freeze in an ice cream maker according to manufacturer's directions. Portion the ice cream into $1/2$-ounce round molds, or using an ice cream scoop, form small balls. Put on a tray in the freezer until ready to serve.

To plate

1. Cut the lamb paper-thin and place a portion on each plate. Top with the onion, capers, chives, croutons, and arugula. In a medium bowl, coat the lettuce with dressing and toss with Parmigiano-Reggiano. Place the lettuce on the plates. Set a few balls of ice cream on top.

SERVES 4 TO 6

PAN-SEARED MAINE DIVER SCALLOPS *with* CARAMELIZED ENDIVE, LEEK PURÉE, *and* SHAVED BLACK TRUFFLE

LEEK PURÉE

1 cup fresh spinach

1 cup sliced leek whites

¼ cup peeled and finely diced russet potato

Kosher salt

Freshly ground black pepper

Sugar

VEAL SAUCE

1 cup veal stock

½ cup chicken stock

RICE VINEGAR SYRUP

¼ cup rice vinegar

¼ cup sugar

ENDIVE

3 heads yellow endive

1 tablespoon olive oil

2 tablespoons unsalted butter

PARMIGIANO-REGGIANO FROTH

2 tablespoons unsalted butter

1 cup freshly grated Parmigiano-Reggiano

1½ teaspoons soy lecithin

SCALLOPS

2 tablespoons clarified butter

6 Maine diver scallops

GARNISHES

Black peppercorns, freshly cracked

Red peppercorns, freshly cracked

Celery heart leaves

Black truffle

To make the leek purée

1. In a 1-quart saucepan of boiling water, blanch the spinach for 30 seconds. Remove, reserving the boiling water, and immediately plunge into ice water. Let cool, remove from the ice water, and dry the spinach on clean towels.

2. Blanch the leeks in the same water for 30 seconds. Remove, reserving the boiling water, plunge into the ice water. Let cool, drain, and dry the leeks.

3. Blanch the potato in the same until fully tender. Drain.

4. Purée the spinach, leek, and potato with a cube of ice in a blender or food processor for 1 to 2 minutes. Pass the mixture through a fine-mesh strainer and return it to the blender or processor. Season with salt, pepper, and sugar.

CONTINUED

To make the veal sauce

1. In a medium saucepan over medium heat, simmer the veal stock until reduced by half, about 30 minutes. Add the chicken stock and reduce this now by one half to $^{1}/_{2}$ cup, simmering about 20 minutes. Remove from the heat and let the sauce cool to room temperature. Pour it into a squeeze bottle and reserve.

To make the rice vinegar syrup

1. Combine the vinegar and sugar in a medium saucepan and bring to a boil. Immediately remove from the heat and reserve.

To make the endive

1. Remove the outer leaves of the endive and cut each head in half lengthwise. Score each half at the base multiple times with a paring knife. In a large skillet or sauté pan over high heat, warm the oil. Sear the endive face down. Lower the heat to medium and add $^{1}/_{2}$ cup of the rice vinegar syrup and the butter. Continue to cook until a light glaze forms that coats the endive, 2 to 3 minutes. The leaves should be soft and "fanable" while leaving a "bite" at the heart. Reserve warm.

To make the froth

1. Combine $^{1}/_{2}$ cup water and the butter in a small saucepan. Heat, but do not boil. Remove from the heat. Add the Parmigiano-Reggiano and soy lecithin. Mix with a hand blender. Adjust the seasoning with salt. Reserve at room temperature.

To make the scallops

1. In a medium skillet or sauté pan over high heat, add the clarified butter and scallops. Sear until golden brown and caramelized, 2 to 3 minutes per side. Transfer the scallops to a plate and let rest for 2 minutes.

To plate

1. Using a spoon or small ladle, spread 2 tablespoons leek purée in a wide stripe down the center of each plate and top with $1^{1}/_{2}$ teaspoons veal sauce. Fan an endive half over the purée. Cut the scallops horizontally into 3 equal parts and fan one scallop onto the sauce on each plate. Add Parmigiano-Reggiano froth to the plates around the scallops. Sprinkle peppercorns over the plate. Place 3 to 5 celery leaves across the plate and shave black truffle over each scallop. Serve immediately.

SERVES 6

2002

LIDIA MATTICCHIO BASTIANICH

CHAPTER *thirteen*

LIDIA MATTICCHIO BASTIANICH IS A LADY TO BE RECKONED WITH. HER LIFE IS A STORY OF AN ITALIAN-BORN IMMIGRANT EMBRACING A FOREIGN LAND, AND THEN ACHIEVING FAME AND ADULATION. The young girl who came here from post—World War II Italy brought with her an appreciation of regional Italian cooking and culture. Her culinary knowledge is a gift that she now shares with millions of Americans through her Emmy-nominated television series and best-selling books.

Bastianich is the matriarch of a business built on passion. She is a restaurateur, chef, television celebrity, and has even been the Grand Marshal of the Columbus Day Parade in New York City. But the titles that matter most to her are daughter, mother, and grandmother. "My mother lives with me; she's ninety. My daughter lives two blocks away. She has two kids. My son has three kids. There's always four generations at my house and, of course, they always ask, 'What are we going to eat?'"

Her two children also play an integral role in the Bastianich businesses and participate in expanding the family empire. She partnered with son Joseph in opening his first restaurant, Becco, in Manhattan. He also operates three Bastianich wineries in Italy: Bastianich winery in Friuli, La Mozza vineyards in Tuscany, and Agricola Brandini in Piedmont. Joe also co-wrote two award-winning books and received two James Beard awards himself, one for wine and the other in partnership with Mario Batali for Babbo, as restaurant of the year. Lidia and Joe are also partners in Lidia's Italy restaurants in Kansas City and Pittsburgh.

Bastianich's daughter, Tanya Bastianich Manuali, holds a doctorate in Renaissance history from Oxford, and partners with her mother in Esperienze Italiane, a travel agency specializing in food, wine, and art tours. They work together on the television series, books, and a product line. "We're all together in business and it's a family business," Bastianich explains.

Lidia's voyage from Italy to the United States was difficult. She was born in 1947 in Istria, a peninsula now part of Croatia, about ninety miles northeast of Venice, an area that fell under communist rule after the war. She fled with her parents and her brother, Franco, to Trieste, Italy, and lived for two years with other displaced families in a refugee camp at the site of a former Nazi concentration camp. "It was really hard," she says. "There weren't any jobs, and there wasn't enough of anything to go around. So my family thought that the best thing would be for us to come to the New World."

A special provision for political refugees allowed the family to emigrate to the United States in 1958 with the help of Catholic Charities in New York. "We had no one. They found a home for us. They found a job for my father."

The family settled in North Bergen, New Jersey, and Bastianich began working in bakeries and restaurants to pay for her education. Although she was studying science, theology, and chemistry with hopes of pursuing a medical career, cooking changed that future.

The mainly self-taught dynamo opened her first restaurant with no prior business experience. As a restaurant chef, Bastianich became one of the first women to break into what had been traditionally a male field.

Bastianich had two successful restaurants in Queens, New York, by 1971, but closed those restaurants to concentrate on one operation. A $750,000 renovation in 1981 turned a Manhattan brownstone into Felidia Ristorante, which featured Bastianich's beloved regional Italian foods. Felidia Ristorante gave Bastianich the chance to reach back to her childhood for cooking memories of her tight-knit family. Food was always the center of her existence and tied her to her grandparents' farm on the outskirts of Istria.

"Understanding food from the ground is the essence of the food and the flavors. It's not about me inventing. Nature does that. It's about me exalting it and having the good sense to harvest it at the perfect time, the perfect maturity, to serve it at the perfect temperature—not cold from the refrigerator, when all the flavors are locked. That's what nature has taught me. Going up on a cherry tree and just picking the ripest cherries, the ones that had a little nip from a bird. I knew that that was the sweetest one because the birds knew better. We climbed fig trees and when the figs were kind of drooping and had little stretch marks with just a drop of honey coming out of the end, we just knew that those were the best ones. These are the flavors I always try to recapture or refine." She explains, "I've brought these memories with me to America and they linger on. It is a way of connecting with my roots, and being a part of the family left behind. Food is such a communicator, such an important part of me, of my story. And I continue to communicate with it."

Felidia Ristorante opened to widespread critical acclaim and quickly received a three-star review from the *New York Times*. "I just did what we cook at home and people loved it," she says, with characteristic modesty. The authentic flavors from her native region changed New Yorkers' views of Italian cuisine. At the same time, it enabled Bastianich to establish a flourishing food and entertainment business. "I am the perfect example," she says, "that if you give somebody a chance, especially here in America, one can find the way."

Her businesses have also been built through friendships. James Beard often dined at Felidia after the restaurant's opening. "I would cook for him, and serve him. We would sit at the table together," Bastianich remembers. She is still fascinated by just how big he was, how hungry he was, and his vast knowledge. "He was instrumental in mobilizing, if you will, the whole movement of food enjoyment, cooking, and sharing." When he died and the idea emerged of keeping his memory and his home alive, Bastianich contributed to the James Beard Foundation and continues to support the organization.

Julia Child gave Bastianich her first national television exposure. She was introduced as part of the 1993 series "Julia Child: Cooking with Master Chefs," taped in Child's kitchen, an experience that twice provided Bastianich lessons in media presentation. "She spoke to engage the audience," Lidia observed. "It wasn't about her."

The setting and the style was a formula Bastianich adopted for her own PBS programs. She also attributes some of her mannerisms on TV and techniques in book writing to Child. As a result, she's natural and warm, and makes the viewer or reader feel welcome to drop into her kitchen for a cappuccino and to chat about dinner. Bastianich's instructions are clear and thoughtful, and her teaching focuses on the process: "It is about people successfully using the recipes."

But cooking is not just a process to Bastianich.

"FOOD IS A WAY OF CONNECTING WITH THE PEOPLE WHO SURROUND US. THROUGH IT, WE COMMUNICATE EMOTIONS LIKE LOVE, COMPASSION, AND UNDERSTANDING, AND THERE IS NO BETTER OPPORTUNITY TO COMMUNICATE WITH OUR CHILDREN THAN AT THE TABLE.

It's where we can discuss our values as individuals, as a family, and as a part of the world."

Bastianich believes that today's cooks could learn from the way previous generations subsisted. "As overconsumption and greed have come to haunt us, now is a time for reflection. We should be looking back at the generations before us to understand their approach to the table. Growing food, shepherding animals, foraging for the gifts of nature are all part of respecting food. Nothing needs to be wasted." She adds, "Respect for the food we prepare also leads to a more sensible and balanced intake of proteins, legumes, and vegetables. So waste not, want not, and make it delicious!"

Bastianich often returns to Italy to research recipes, cooking techniques, and ingredients to broaden her knowledge. "My recipes are all part of the Italian patrimony. And my trips to Italy, every single time, reveal to me mounds of recipes. There's plenty to be had there," she notes.

Recently, she joined her son and Mario Batali in the Eataly venture, heading up the cooking school there—La Scuola di Eataly.

The proud grandmother of five believes that it's not only the food on the table that makes the meal; people who join around the table bring the meal to life. *Tutti a tavola a mangiare!*—Everybody to the table to eat!—is a refrain that has been repeated in Italian households for centuries.

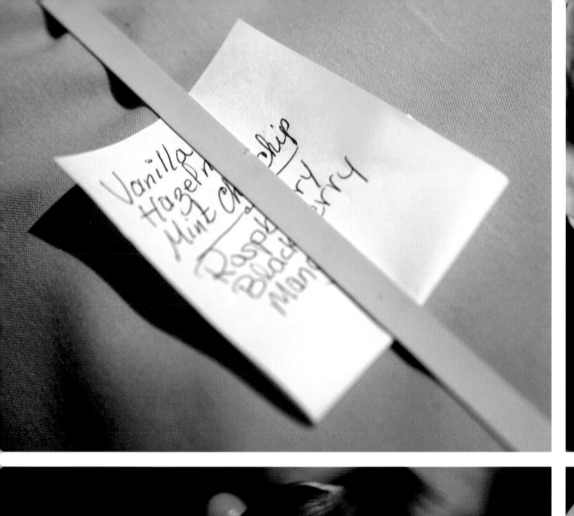

PACCHERI *with* ANNA SANTORO'S PESTO TRAPANESE

Paccheri al Pesto Trapanese di Anna Santoro

2½ cups very ripe cherry tomatoes (about 12 ounces)

⅓ cup whole almonds, lightly toasted

12 large fresh whole basil leaves

1 plump garlic clove, crushed and peeled

¼ teaspoon pepperoncini flakes

½ teaspoon coarse sea salt or kosher salt, plus salt for cooking pasta

½ cup extra-virgin olive oil, plus more if needed

1 pound paccheri pasta

1 pound small shrimp, peeled and deveined

½ cup grated fresh Grana Padano or Parmigiano-Reggiano cheese

1. To the bowl of a food processor or blender jar, add the tomatoes, almonds, basil, garlic, pepperoncini, and salt. Purée, scraping down the sides. With the machine running, stream in the oil, emulsifying the purée into a thick pesto. Adjust the seasoning.

2. Cook the paccheri according to the package directions.

3. When the pasta is al dente, add the shrimp, stir, and turn off the heat. Let stand for 1 minute. Drain the paccheri, reserving ½ cup of the cooking water. Return the pasta and shrimp to the pot and fold in the pesto until all the pasta is coated with the pesto. Optionally, drizzle in extra-virgin olive oil and some of the reserved pasta water, if needed. Sprinkle with the cheese and toss. Serve immediately in warmed bowls.

SERVES 4 TO 6

SPICY CALAMARI *Calamari Piccanti*

2 pounds cleaned calamari, whole bodies and tentacles, skin on or off

3/4 cup extra-virgin olive oil, divided

6 garlic cloves, crushed

1½ teaspoons kosher salt, divided

½ teaspoon pepperoncini flakes

2 tablespoons fresh lemon juice

1 tablespoon chopped fresh Italian parsley

1. To a large bowl, add the calamari, ½ cup of the oil, the garlic, 1 teaspoon of the salt, and the pepperoncini. Toss to coat and marinate at room temperature for 30 to 60 minutes.

2. To make the dressing, in a small bowl, whisk the remaining ¼ cup olive oil, the lemon juice, remaining ½ teaspoon salt, and the parsley until emulsified.

3. Drain the calamari briefly.

4. In a 12-inch sauté pan or skillet over high heat, sear the calamari in batches, turning several times until crispy with caramelized edges, about 2 minutes. The skin will darken to a deep-reddish hue. Arrange on a warmed platter to reserve while searing the remainder of the calamari.

5. When all the calamari are plated, drizzle with the dressing. Serve immediately.

SERVES 6

LIMONCELLO TIRAMISÙ

5 large eggs

1 cup sugar, divided

1½ cups limoncello liqueur, divided

¾ cup fresh lemon juice

2 cups mascarpone cheese,
at room temperature (about 1 pound)

2 tablespoons grated lemon zest

40 ladyfingers, preferably imported
Italian Savoiardi, or more as needed

Candied kumquats, for garnish (optional)

Fine shreds of lemon zest, for garnish

To make the zabaglione base

1. Separate the eggs, putting the yolks into the top of a double boiler or in a large bowl. Reserve the whites for whipping. Beat the yolks with ¼ cup of the sugar and ½ cup of the limoncello. Mix well.

2. Heat water in a saucepan to a steady simmer. Set the yolks over the simmering water, whisking constantly and scraping the sides, until the egg mixture expands to a frothy sponge, 5 minutes or longer. When the sponge has thickened enough to form ribbons, remove and let it cool.

To make the tiramisù

1. To a large saucepan over high heat, add the remaining 1 cup limoncello, the lemon juice, 1 cup water, and ½ cup of the sugar. Boil, stirring to dissolve the sugar, for 5 minutes. Let the syrup cool completely.

2. In another large bowl, stir the mascarpone with a wooden spoon to soften. Add the lemon zest and beat until light and creamy.

3. Using a mixer or by hand, whip the egg whites with the remaining ¼ cup sugar until the egg whites hold moderately firm peaks.

CONTINUED

4. When the zabaglione is cooled, scrape one third of it over the mascarpone and fold it in with a large rubber spatula. Fold in the rest of the zabaglione in 2 or 3 additions. Fold in the egg whites in several additions, until the limoncello-mascarpone cream is light and evenly blended.

5. Into a 9-by-13-inch glass baking dish, pour ¼ inch cooled syrup. Working one at a time, roll 20 of the ladyfingers quickly in the syrup and place them in the dish, arranging in neat, tight rows. They should fill the bottom of the dish completely.

6. Cover with half of the limoncello-mascarpone cream. Dip the remaining ladyfingers in syrup and arrange a second layer of ladyfingers in the dish. Cover with the remaining cream.

7. Smooth the cream with a spatula and seal the tiramisù airtight in plastic wrap. Refrigerate for 6 hours or freeze for 2 hours. It may be kept in the refrigerator for up to 2 days.

To plate
1. To serve, cut the tiramisù into squares or use a 2- to 2½-inch ring mold to cut out circular portions. Garnish each serving with candied kumquats, if using, and shreds of lemon zest.

SERVES 12 OR MORE

2003

ERIC RIPERT

CHAPTER *fourteen*

A FORTUNE-TELLER ONCE PROMISED ERIC RIPERT THAT HE WOULD SOMEDAY BE A CHEF IN A GREAT RESTAURANT. Perhaps it's no coincidence, then, that the world's highest-profile seafood chef has a cat named Mystic.

Ripert is executive chef and co-owner of the Manhattan restaurant Le Bernardin. The restaurant exemplifies the international standard of progressive French seafood. He's content, watching his kitchen move in Zen-like harmony, a graceful corps de ballet of cooks. Focused tranquility is important to someone who has practiced Buddhism for more than twenty years.

Fate intervened earlier than predicted, though. He bought a book about Buddhism from a train station rack. Intrigued, he began his travels toward self-discovery and a meteoric rise as a chef.

"The way I see life, everything is spiritual," he says. "We live on Earth, we are omnivores, the nature of human beings is to eat meat and fruits and vegetables, and therefore we have to kill animals. I don't have a problem with that. But it's a sacred moment."

As an owner of an exalted establishment that elevates fish to haute cuisine standards, does Ripert fish? "No," he smiles with a Gallic shrug. He does a much better job of cooking them.

Ripert buoyantly followed a vocational rather than a scholastic career. "Why did I need to know when the train leaves Paris and another one leaves Lyon?" he asks. "And, where are they going to cross each other? I could have cared less about that train," he laughs. "I care about food."

The chef first learned to cook from his grandmother, absorbing her Mediterranean style. He then entered culinary school when he was fifteen in Perpignan, France, not far from the family home in Andorra, Spain.

Following graduation, Ripert sent letters to all the three-star Michelin restaurants in France. He received only one response: a "no" from Maxim's. Several weeks later, though, someone from the legendary, 400-year-old restaurant La Tour d'Argent called on a Friday. Ripert was in Paris by Monday morning. He started in *garde-manger,* running home at lunchtime to practice his knife skills.

In 1984 he joined Joël Robuchon at Jamin, another three-star Michelin restaurant in Paris. At Jamin, Ripert worked his way up to *chef poissonnier*—fish chef, with a brief hiatus for military duty. "You need to be a good technician," he says of cooking seafood. "I love how very delicate fish is—you have to treat it in a very subtle way."

Robuchon was a magnificent influence on Ripert, who learned discipline and structure in the older man's kitchen. The protégé was rewarded with irresistible opportunities.

Robuchon helped Ripert move to the United States in 1989 as sous-chef with the late Jean-Louis Palladin at the Watergate Hotel in Washington, D.C. Palladin taught Ripert to have fun in a less formal kitchen and to riff on the classics. For a chef trained in the dogma of French recipes, Palladin's approach was liberating. "He pushed me to kill the fear to express myself," Ripert acknowledges. "He freed my mind."

Two years later, he moved to New York as a sous-chef under David Bouley, but quickly went to Le Bernardin. There he became the chef, working with Gilbert Le Coze and Maguy Le Coze, the restaurant's glamorous brother and sister team. A close friendship with Gilbert gave Ripert carte blanche as chef, although Gilbert told him "to keep in mind there is a soul of Le Bernardin. Don't do something that is against those principles." Then he let Ripert make all the mistakes he wanted. What Gilbert really did, though, was allow Ripert to advance from a chef who merely cooked to one who managed the kitchen—he afforded Ripert a higher level of knowledge and experience. And he taught Ripert that a great cook must also be a great leader.

Gilbert died unexpectedly from a heart attack in 1994, leaving Maguy Le Coze and Ripert to manage by themselves. Maguy Le Coze's natural élan continued distinguishing the front of the house, and with the kitchen now under control, Ripert became co-owner.

Ripert cares intensely about the restaurant, the people who work there, the guest experience, and the purveyors. Many of Le Bernardin's crew have been there for over a decade, anchoring management with little turnover in important positions.

Le Bernardin has fostered three other restaurants by Ripert: Blue in the Cayman Islands (a AAA five-diamond restaurant), West End Bistro in Washington, D.C., and 10 Arts in Philadelphia. "Those chefs, they were each here with me at Le Bernardin," says Ripert.

Ripert manages his kitchen with a classic hierarchy, based on the French brigade tradition. The sous-chefs take responsibility for the *commis*—young cooks learning a craft, including interns, externs, and visiting cooks doing a stage.

The restaurant's suppliers are longtime purveyors integral to the standards at Le Bernardin. Ripert insists that a very good relationship with purveyors is important. "Therefore, we get the fish first. We pay the fair price and we pay very, very quickly," he acknowledges. "This is a sign of respect and if you go to a fish market right now and look for black bass you're not going to find any. However, in the back of a truck somewhere is the black bass for Le Bernardin."

Ripert is always reaching and growing to another level. Recently he launched a PBS series, *Avec Eric*, which follows his travels around the world, exploring locations where food and tradition come together to create special dining experiences. He has made several guest appearances on cooking-based television shows, including guest judge and assistant chef roles on four seasons of Bravo's *Top Chef*.

Ripert has also appeared on many episodes of Anthony Bourdain's show *No Reservations*, and played himself in a segment of the television series *Treme*, based in New Orleans.

While the demands of celebrity chef status eat up a growing number of hours, he says 70 percent of his time is still spent with a stove. "It's a tough balance," he says, "but my priority is to be in the kitchen.

IT'S A VERY DIFFICULT JOB AND IT'S NOT GLAMOROUS. IT'S A VERY REPETITIVE LONG PROCESS, PHYSICAL, DEMANDING, AND A LOT OF SACRIFICE. THAT'S WHAT YOU HAVE TO LOOK AT. HOW MUCH PASSION DO YOU HAVE?"

Ripert totally separates his private life from his professional life and protects the privacy of his family. "When I work, I work," he says. "When I'm with the family, I think about them. When I'm alone, it's time for something I like to do or to reflect."

In his rare time alone, he loves to listen to jazz and blues. He explains, "My cooking at home is very instinctive, and therefore it's very similar to jazz. I improvise at times. Obviously, I have my base but I improvise all the time."

And his base is what keeps it all together, what collects Ripert's intensity and turns it into a cutting tool. He points out, "At Le Bernardin, I end up with the same result. Consistency. What is important is to have the same result for the client—the same sauce, everyday. To get the same sauce you don't have to rethink it every time, you have to know that the products may be different—even made differently. If the tomatoes have too much water, you don't cook them as though they were ripe. So, it's always a bit of improvisation. However, I try to be consistent as much as I can. I tell my cooks, 'Just connect with the act of cooking and the ingredients.' It's almost like meditation but it's very free."

He once told an interviewer that if he were a fish he would be a dolphin. "A dolphin is very friendly, very nice, a free animal," says Ripert with a laugh. "He swims and is a beautiful animal; I don't mean aesthetically, it's beautiful in terms of personality."

He smiles. "I like the symbolism. My sign is Pisces; I'm from the Mediterranean. The dolphin in Greece is a sign of good luck. And I think I bring good luck to people."

STUFFED ZUCCHINI FLOWERS *with* PEEKYTOE *and* KING CRAB *and* FINES HERBES-LEMON MOUSSELINE SAUCE

FINES HERBES–LEMON MOUSSELINE SAUCE

2 egg yolks

3 tablespoons fresh lemon juice

1¼ cups unsalted butter, melted and hot

Fine sea salt

Freshly ground black pepper

1 tablespoon chopped fresh parsley

1 tablespoon chopped fresh chervil

1 tablespoon sliced fresh tarragon

1 tablespoon sliced fresh chives

ZUCCHINI FLOWER AND CRAB FILLING

4 ounces peekytoe crabmeat, picked over

2 tablespoons crème fraîche

1 tablespoon thinly sliced fresh chives

½ teaspoon grated lemon zest

Fresh lemon juice

Freshly ground white pepper

Piment d'Espelette

4 large zucchini flowers, stamens removed

6 ounces shelled king crab leg meat

GARNISHES

½ cup blanched English peas and/or fava beans

¼ cup baby pea tendrils

To make the sauce

1. In a blender, combine the egg yolks and lemon juice and process on medium speed. With the motor running, drizzle the butter into the blender in a steady stream. When fully incorporated, season with salt and pepper and transfer to a sauce pan to keep warm.

To make the filling

1. Combine the peekytoe crabmeat, crème fraîche, chives, and lemon zest in a bowl. Season with lemon juice, salt, pepper, and piment d'Espelette. Fill each zucchini flower three-quarters full with stuffing.

2. Cut the king crab meat into 4 pieces. Place the stuffed zucchini flowers and the king crab in a bamboo steamer. Place a large pot filled with 2 inches of water over high heat and bring it to a boil. Place the steamer over the pot, cover, and steam until the filling is hot, about 3 minutes.

3. While the stuffed zucchini flowers and crab are heating, stir the parsley, chervil, tarragon, and chives into the sauce.

4. To serve, place each zucchini flower on a plate along with a piece of king crab and spoon the sauce over and around the stuffed flower and crab. Garnish with peas and pea tendrils. Serve immediately.

SERVES 4

LOBSTER CITRUS *à la* NAGE

CITRUS NAGE

½ cup champagne vinegar

2 tablespoons sugar

2 lemons

4 tablespoons cold unsalted butter, cut into cubes

Fine sea salt

Freshly ground white pepper

2 tablespoons Mandarin olive oil (see Note)

PICKLED GOLDEN BEETS

2 or 3 golden beets, depending on size

2 cups red wine vinegar

½ cup kosher salt

BAKED LOBSTER

1 cup unsalted butter, cut into large dice

4 lobster tails

4 lobster claws (poached to medium rare and taken out of the shell)

GARNISHES

1 bulb baby fennel, shaved thin

½ grapefruit, peeled, segmented, and diced fine

Olive oil

To make the nage

1. In a small pot, bring 1 cup water, the vinegar, and sugar to a boil. While the vinegar is boiling, wash and zest the lemons and juice them. Add the juice and zest to the vinegar mixture and transfer to the refrigerator for at least 24 hours.

To make the beets

1. Combine 1 quart water, the beets, vinegar, and salt in a medium pot and simmer until the beets are tender, about 40 minutes. Drain the beets and let them cool. Peel the beets and cut them horizontally into ⅛-inch slices. Trim each slice into a 1-inch circle with a round cutter. Lay the beet circles on a parchment paper–lined baking sheet. The beets can be cooked and sliced ahead of time and kept refrigerated until ready to use.

CONTINUED

To make the lobster

1. Preheat the oven to 450°F. Make a *beurre monté* by bringing ¼ cup water to a boil. Whisk in the butter in a couple of increments; season with salt and pepper and keep warm.

2. Put the lobster tails in a pan and bake until cooked through, 8 to 10 minutes.

3. Remove the beets from refrigeration and season them with salt and pepper. Lightly warm the beets in the oven for about 5 minutes. Meanwhile, drop the lobster claws into the warm *beurre monté* to heat.

4. Strain the nage into a small pot and bring it to a simmer over medium heat. Whisk in the cold butter 1 tablespoon at a time, until the nage is emulsified. Season with salt and pepper and finish the nage with the oil.

To plate

1. Arrange 5 slices of beets, slightly overlapping, on one side of each plate. Take the lobster tails out of their shells and slice them into 5 slices each. Arrange the lobster tail slices parallel to the beets. Place a claw on top of the sliced beets on each plate. Lightly dress the shaved fennel and grapefruit with olive oil, salt, and pepper. Garnish the tails with 2 slices of fennel and some diced grapefruit. Spoon the nage over and around the lobster and serve immediately.

NOTE: Mandarin olive oil is olive oil that has been infused with the natural oils in Mandarin oranges. It is available in many specialty food stores and online.

SERVES 4

2004

JUDY RODGERS

CHAPTER *Fifteen*

WHEN A BEAUTIFUL WOMAN IS ALSO A FAMOUS, CELEBRATED CHEF, LIFE IS RARELY FRAUGHT WITH GLAMOUR. With No. 2 pencils securing her topknot and a notepad or a menu not far away, Judy Rodgers records an idea almost as quickly as the flash that arouses her imagination, whether it's a suggestion to make her menu a little more appetizing or just a thought about keeping the customers happy. Rodgers's lifelong habit of note-taking is a key component to her success as a chef and restaurateur.

The influence of traditional French and Italian cooking in her menus at Zuni Café in San Francisco, California, came from recipes she copied and notes she took while eating or observing chefs at work in some of the world's most famous restaurants, beginning when she was a teenager. Rodgers signed on as chef at Zuni Café in 1987, highlighting the restaurant's eclectic status with a menu that continues to dominate San Francisco's casual dining scene more than two decades later.

Zuni Café is housed in a pie-shaped wedge of a building in San Francisco's Hayes Valley, where vintage trolleys rattle past, pedestrians amble under the restaurant's bright yellow awnings, and guests sip cocktails outside on a lazy afternoon. Rodgers is as high-spirited and down-to-earth as the restaurant. Willowy and fast moving, she talks with her hands and punctuates by bringing forefingers and thumbs together in an arcing exclamation.

"The quiet and often shy Judy that we see in the dining room at Zuni Café changes into a not-so-shy and by-no-means-quiet dynamo in the kitchen," says co-owner Gilbert Pilgram. "That is what has allowed the restaurant to become what some customers describe as 'the town square of San Francisco' while keeping the food simple, fad-free, and satisfying." Pilgram worked at Chez Panisse for twenty years. He retired and then became bored. Now, he teams up with Rodgers in the kitchen and oversees the front of the house with bonhomie.

Creating a friendly atmosphere and keeping a menu of simple food that defies trendiness is a lesson Rodgers took to heart from French and Italian restaurateurs, one that keeps on attracting customers. Inside Zuni Café, a wood-burning oven situated between the open kitchen, dining areas, and bar, is used to toast bread, roast Zuni's famous chicken, bake thin-crust pizzas, and prepare many other specialties.

For Rodgers, cooking is about more than just making food that tastes good:

"AS A CHEF, EACH TIME I SHOP FOR, MAKE, AND TASTE A DISH, I AM REVIVING AND MAYBE REINVENTING MY OWN HISTORY WITH THE DISH AND ITS INGREDIENTS, BUT I AM ALSO THINKING ABOUT HOW IT WILL BE RECEIVED.

Every diner brings different memories and tastes to the table. I feel lucky to share some of my favorite ones. We have our repertoire. It's very seasonal and product-based. But for me, so much with cooking has to do with the experience at the table—the cultural experience, the notion of conviviality. When I taste a dish and look at a dish, as much as anything I am wondering how it will be received. Will they embrace the dish? Will it feel fun, easy, or challenging? Will it delight? Will the guests take a bite and want another?" She continues, "It's been very satisfying to have a restaurant in an era and a place where, shockingly, this relatively easy, natural way of cooking is appreciated and esteemed and admired. But, there is a huge irony that here I sit, roasting some chickens. It's just a distillation of paying attention to a lot of traditional cooking and how people made food good. And it's not my originality or Zuni's originality. It's just recognizing how that fits into the lifestyle of San Francisco."

Rodgers says the most difficult years for a restaurateur or young chef are the early ones when he or she must determine what to cook, what he or she is good at, and what he or she wants the restaurant to be. "I knew in a heartbeat what I wanted Zuni to be, but it took years of experimentation, and expanding Zuni's repertoire." In the process, she logged and documented everything: The keepers. The losers. "Over the decades, the repertory has grown, and we constantly revise and refine our methods, but there was a moment that I realized that the pressure to constantly add new dishes and combinations wasn't really necessary. We sort of had our own traditions at Zuni. It was a great relief," she now says as an original proponent of the California culinary movement.

"I don't think it's all about having the best food. What's more, the 'best' is infinitely disputable," Rodgers says. Much of Zuni's charm has to do with the experience at the table. She's especially interested in the cultural experience, and a guest's emotional response. "A dish should be lovely, but I want it to satisfy and promote conviviality as well. Food that kind of creates silence and awe? I don't know how to do that."

Rodgers's note-taking began when, as a sixteen-year-old exchange student in France, she traded places with the daughter of the famous Troisgros family of Les Frères Troisgros. Rodgers lived above their restaurant in Roanne as a member of the family. They nurtured her interest in their regional food and the culinary ethics and aesthetics of France's most revered establishments.

"I was really very attracted to the simpler food, the traditional food, and started paying attention to the two chefs, their sister, and their aunt. They saw how interested I was and they put a lot of energy into teaching me and exposing me to the foods of the region. So, I would go to their aunt's house and she would make all the traditional dishes. They took me to small restaurants, to markets to wineries, and cellars," recalls Rodgers.

The neighbor who arranged the yearlong exchange with the Troisgros's daughter asked Rodgers to chronicle the recipes she experienced in France as her thank-you. Rodgers has always felt that she got the best of the swap between the two girls. Rodgers says, "That was all he asked for in return, so I took it to heart." The result is volumes of lists documenting the food from that area of Burgundy in 1973 and 1974.

Rodgers had Jean Troisgros double-check the accuracy of the recipes she was excited about. "I wrote them and re-wrote them—I have them all, still. When I came home, I translated them all into English, made multiple copies."

One set of copies went into a safe deposit box. "It was quite lucky that I was asked to record those recipes. The process forced me to pay ever more attention to the cooks, the ingredients, and the methods. In particular, I learned from seeing the same dishes made every day at Troisgros. Jean would go out of his way to explain why he was using less cream today because it was thicker, or more lemon, because it was less acidic than usual. He always gave me the reason." At Troisgros, the emphasis was on the importance of ingredients, the foundation that Rodgers builds upon by assuring Zuni Café has the best fresh-farm products.

Rodgers had returned to America with a heightened interest in cooking and was motivated to share the traditional foods of France that were so much a part of her own culinary history. It was a stint at Chez Panisse that jump-started Rodgers' professional food career. Rodgers first heard about Chez Panisse during her senior year at Stanford University, where she received a degree in art history. A friend, who was a server there, told Rodgers about the restaurant. The server had also told Chez Panisse owner Alice Waters she had a friend who had spent a summer at Troisgros and had written down all the recipes. Rodgers had dinner at the restaurant, talked with Waters, and they discovered many common interests. "I had lived a fabulous year at Troisgros and I missed and craved that ambiance and energy. I sensed that same delicious, seductive energy at Chez Panisse."

Waters was planning a sabbatical and needed someone to fill in for her cooking lunch. Although Rodgers had little to no experience actually working in a restaurant, Waters asked her to try out for the job. She auditioned there after spring break.

Rodgers had no thoughts about committing herself to being a chef or restaurateur. "I just sort of happened into it, by being placed in France at the best restaurant in the world, and then coming to Northern California—the perfect spot, at the perfect moment—to capitalize on that experience."

After working for a week at Chez Panisse in the spring of 1977, Rodgers was hired and began her two-year stint as lunch chef. Rodgers says she "kind of winged it" every day during her first few weeks on the job because of her inexperience. "I would write a menu and Alice would come in and troubleshoot, and believe me, there was some trouble to shoot. But gradually, I figured out how to do some basic things to pull it off, not the least of which was to taste, and taste, and taste."

"She has a beautiful artistic sense about food," says Alice Waters. "It's very rare to find cooks that are artists, and also artists who are cooks. This is a sensibility that I really appreciate, and inspires me. She just puts it on the plate in a very different way." After Waters returned, Rodgers took her own sabbatical in Europe to figure out her next career move. Some old friends suggested that on her way to Spain she stop in a tiny village south of Bordeaux to see their friend Pepette Arbulo.

She ended up staying the whole summer at Pepette's rustic restaurant, L'Estanquet, learning the food of southwest France. As she recounts, "It was the pure, minimal, regional restaurant, serving just things from that region in 'un-falutin' interpretations that were Pepette's distillation of her heritage. We would go to the farm and pick up the foie gras. There were no trucks, no deliveries. That drove home what Jean Troisgros had talked about. What you eat every day is just as important as fancy restaurant food. Unadulterated regional fare—the dishes that are ubiquitous and delicious in countless forms in a given region—these culinary repertories are cultural treasures, sustainable and sustaining over generations."

With the real country restaurant experience now part of her background, Rodgers returned to California as chef with Marion Cunningham. She developed a menu of simple and traditional American dishes at the Union Hotel in Benicia, California.

"Endless fried chicken, acres of spoonbread, countless cream biscuits, 6-hour Indian pudding. But the most important thing was not the dishes. I obsessed over Native American ingredients—wild rice, fiddleheads, wild persimmons, miners' lettuce, ramps, and I was enchanted by the quality of local produce that was becoming available. I was certain there was nowhere better in the world to be cooking."

She worked to find innovative ways to produce dishes and recipes similar to what she had experienced in France. In 1983, Rodgers rented a farmhouse outside Florence, Italy, and once again began to write down everything she ate, cooked, and found for sale at the local markets. After subsequent trips through many other parts of Italy, Rodgers returned to California with a significant goal: to settle down at a restaurant that would allow her to cook and share the traditional foods of France and Italy that were so much a part of her own culinary history.

She landed at the Zuni Café in 1987 as chef and ultimately became co-owner. For Rodgers, Zuni is all about running just one restaurant, keeping a small and tight operation, serving good food, and creating a happy environment.

Considering the multiple honors and accolades she has received as a chef and as an author, Rodgers keeps a low profile. Her No. 2 pencils came in handy again, when she wrote a cookbook, now a classic. "Since it was published in 2002, I've watched *The Zuni Café Cookbook* take its place in the pantheon of great cookbooks," says Maria Guarnaschelli, senior editor and vice president, W. W. Norton. "It's more than a treasure trove of great recipes. It's also an important series of insights on cooking written in beautiful prose."

Rodgers and her "fabulous partner," Pilgram, share culinary tastes and backgrounds and have one common goal for Zuni Café: "We both are attracted to restaurants and hotels that are personally run by the owner. We want our restaurant to feel like our home and reflect our taste not just in food, but architecture, paintings, music, all those things that come naturally after living for many years in a house. This includes a few defects and imperfections that we have come to embrace like the 100-year-old windows that are a project to keep clean but provide a beautiful light. We just want this restaurant to be as good as possible."

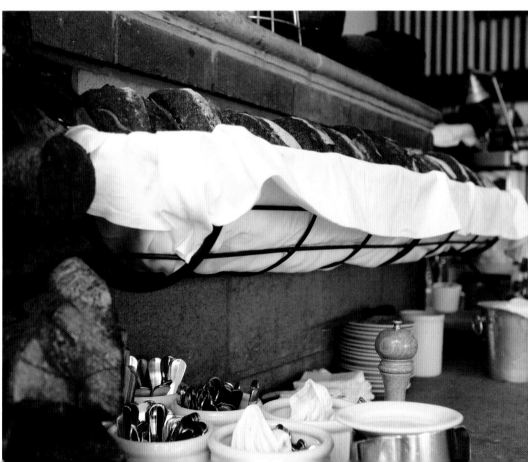

"SALMON BACON," LETTUCE *and* TOMATO SANDWICH

3 to 4 ounces salmon belly, skinned

¼ teaspoon salt

½ teaspoon coarse cracked black pepper

2 slices country-style white bread or chewy *levain* bread, about ½ inch thick

1 teaspoon plus 1 tablespoon extra-virgin olive oil

1 teaspoon red wine vinegar

Tender lettuce leaves
(to cover a slice of bread in two layers)

About 3 ounces room-temperature tender, ripe tomatoes (your favorite heirloom variety), sliced ¼ inch thick

1 to 2 tablespoons homemade aioli or lemon mayonnaise or anchovy mayonnaise (optional)

4 large shiso leaves

1. One day in advance, toss the salmon belly with the salt and pepper, place on plate, cover loosely, and refrigerate.

2. The next day, choose a nonstick or well-seasoned cast-iron pan just wide enough to accommodate the belly in one layer. Cut the belly into a few pieces if necessary.

3. Set the pan on medium heat, warm it until the fish sizzles on contact, and then lay all the fish neatly in the pan. Leave to sizzle and cook undisturbed as it renders its fat and turns golden and crunchy on the bottom, about 5 minutes. Don't let the salmon burn, but likewise, turn up the heat if it isn't beginning to color within a few minutes. Carefully turn it over to crisp and color the other side, a few minutes at most. The salmon should have a firm golden crust and will be cooked through, but will remain succulent and flavorful, owing to its natural richness and the brief salt cure.

4. Meanwhile, brush the slices of bread with 1 teaspoon of the oil and lightly toast under the broiler, in a toaster oven, or on the grill.

5. Combine the remaining 1 tablespoon oil and the vinegar with a pinch of salt to make a tart vinaigrette. Toss the lettuce in the vinaigrette. Lightly season the tomatoes with salt.

6. Slather one of the slices of still-warm bread with aioli, if using. Layer with the cool lettuce leaves, overlapping tomato slices, the *shiso*, and then the warm, crispy salmon. Top with the second slice of bread.

7. Eat immediately.

SERVES 1

FRISÉE *and* ESCAROLE SALAD *with* GOLDEN RAISINS, SUNCHOKES, DRY JACK CHEESE, AND ALMONDS

¼ cup golden raisins

6 tablespoons dry sherry

1 small shallot, finely diced

1½ tablespoons red wine vinegar

6 tablespoons extra-virgin olive oil

Salt

6 ounces small, tender frisée and escarole leaves

20 almonds, toasted and very coarsely chopped

2 ounces sunchoke, washed and trimmed, but not peeled

1 to 2 ounces dry Jack cheese, rind removed

Freshly cracked black pepper

1. At least 3 days before you make the salad, combine the raisins and sherry in a small jar, cover, and leave at room temperature. Shake the jar a little each day to encourage the raisins to absorb the sherry evenly. They should absorb all or nearly all the sherry.

2. Combine the shallots and vinegar in a small bowl and set aside to marinate. After about 20 minutes, whisk in the oil and season with salt.

3. Drain the raisins.

4. Place the frisée and escarole in a large salad bowl. Add the almonds and raisins. Using a vegetable peeler or mandoline, shave the sunchoke into thin slices onto the greens. Next, shave about 1 ounce of the cheese into the bowl. Add the vinaigrette and toss well to make sure every leaf is fully coated with dressing. Taste and add salt, if needed.

5. Divide the salad among four small plates, dividing the elements evenly. Garnish each salad with shavings of the remaining cheese and finish with a few grinds of black pepper.

SERVES 4

BREAD SOUP

4 tablespoons extra-virgin olive oil, divided

½ cup ¼-inch dice carrot (4 ounces)

½ cup ¼-inch dice celery (4 ounces)

½ cup ¼-inch dice yellow onion (4 ounces)

½ cup green beans or Romano beans, cut into ½-inch pieces (4 ounces)

Salt

½ cup ¼-inch dice summer squash (4 ounces) (see Note)

½ cup 1-inch pieces deribbed Swiss chard leaves (4 ounces)

½ cup peeled, coarsely chopped, ripe Early Girl or Roma tomatoes (4 ounces)

½ cup cooked salted shelling beans, such as cannellini, flageolet, garbanzo, or cranberry beans (4 ounces)

6 ounces chewy-stale white country-style bread (ciabatta works well)

4 cups rich chicken stock, lightly salted

16 basil leaves, torn into ½-inch pieces

Freshly cracked black pepper

Parmigiano-Reggiano, Gruyère, or aged Tuscan pecorino cheese, grated (optional)

1. In a heavy bottomed 4-quart pot over medium heat, warm about 2 tablespoons of the oil. Add the carrot, celery, onions, green beans, and a few pinches of salt. Cook gently, stirring occasionally so none of the vegetables brown. If they begin to sizzle aggressively or crackle, reduce the heat. Cook evenly until they are al dente, no longer raw-tasting, but not tender, mushy, or discolored, about 7 minutes. Next, add the squash, chard, tomatoes, another splash of oil, and another pinch of salt. Continue cooking gently until the chard is just limp and the tomatoes are hot through, another few minutes or so. Now all of the vegetables should be just-cooked, with no trace of raw or grassy flavor. Taste for salt as needed.

2. While the vegetables are cooking, drain the shelling beans and set aside their liquid. Carve all of the bottom crust off the bread, then shave off the top and side crusts as well, leaving a bit of the golden inner crust intact. Tear the crusted bread into irregular pieces, ranging in size from fat crumbs to 2-inch pieces. You should have about 5 ounces of bread pieces.

CONTINUED

3. Add the drained shelled beans, 3 cups of the stock, the basil, and the remaining oil to the pot with the vegetables. Raise the heat to medium and stir a few times as the soup comes to a simmer. Taste again for salt and reduce the heat slightly. Cook until all the vegetables are tender, which may take as little as a few minutes or up to 10.

4. Now add 4 ounces of the prepared bread. It should readily absorb into the liquid. Gradually add the remaining stock or substitute some bean cooking liquor if you like that flavor. Stir occasionally as the soup comes to a slow simmer. The soup will be dense. The big and small chunks of bread should be saturated with broth but still intact. Cook for a few more minutes, until the soup starts to thicken. If you drag a spoon across the bottom of the pot, the liquid should slowly ooze back to the center of the pot. If the liquid is still watery, reduce the heat and simmer a few more minutes, until it thickens more, or fold in some—or all—of the remaining bread. If the soup is too dry, add more stock or bean liquor a tablespoon at a time until the texture is dense but succulent. Reseason if necessary.

5. Serve in hot bowls with a generous splash of extra-virgin olive oil and freshly cracked black pepper. It is delicious with freshly grated cheese, if desired.

NOTE: Use pale green varieties of summer squash, such as Lebanese, Cousa, pattypan, or Rond de Nice.

SERVES 6 TO 8

2005

MARIO BATALI

CHAPTER *sixteen*

IT COMES AS NO SURPRISE THAT THE GOOD-NATURED, BARREL-CHESTED, GARRULOUS CHEF MARIO BATALI HELD DOWN HIS FIRST COOKING GIG AT STUFF YER FACE, A PIZZA JOINT IN BRUNSWICK, NEW JERSEY. Like the proverbial pizza man who flings his dough with gusto, Batali tosses zest and zeal into his work.

Batali, born in Yakima, Washington, in 1960, grew up in suburban Seattle. His father, an engineer for Boeing, was transferred to Madrid when Mario was fifteen and Spain was blossoming socially, artistically, and gastronomically. Batali is fluent in Spanish as well as in Italian. He returned to the United States to major in Spanish language, theater, and economics at Rutgers University. Six months after graduation in 1982, Batali was still working at Stuff Yer Face, hooked on the adrenaline rush cooks get when a restaurant goes into dinner service. His work ethic is still fueled by that feeling. When his mother suggested that he consider cooking school, Batali recalled responding, "That's for sissies." A music lover and amateur guitarist, he was more interested in mastering guitar licks than fine-tuning his kitchen skills.

Nonetheless, Batali enrolled at the Cordon Bleu in London, only to drop out a few weeks later because he found the pace too slow. Not taking the full course was a decision he calls "stupid." He says now, "You should finish what you do." Instead of formal culinary training, Batali followed a brutal on-the-job regimen to earn chef status. He was an assistant in the kitchen at a pub in Kings Road, Chelsea, under Marco Pierre White, who would later revolutionize the British restaurant scene. Then Batali did turns at La Tour d'Argent in Paris, Moulin de Mougins in Provence, and the Waterside Inn, outside London.

Returning to the United States in 1985, he worked as a sous-chef at the Four Seasons Clift Hotel in San Francisco, then at La Marina restaurant in Santa Barbara. He was fascinated by California's "New American Cuisine" and landed a job with Jeremiah Tower at Stars, who Batali credits for providing him with much inspiration. Jeremiah Tower describes Mario as a "genius in knowing exactly what the public wants and then doing it—several times."

In 1989, Batali headed to Italy at the age of twenty-nine to learn more about his family's culinary heritage. The few months he planned to stay turned into three years. "Apprenticing at La Volta in Borgo Capanne, Italy, changed my life," says Batali.

In Italy, Mario immersed himself in some of the traditions of Italian cooking that he had learned from his beloved grandmother, Leonetta Merlino, whose ravioli, he says, is legendary. "It's in women's nature to be better at cooking because they don't cook to compete. They cook to feed people," Batali asserts. "Back in Italy, the best chefs are never dudes—it's always the grandma." He often says he strives to cook like an Italian grandmother—nurturing and contagious with joy and hospitality.

For a young chef who arrived in Manhattan in 1992 with just $250 in his pocket, enthusiasm, talent, and a bunch of old T-shirts, he's parlayed his assets into an impressive portfolio of food-related enterprises.

In 1993, Batali and Joseph Bastianich, son of Lidia Bastianich, opened the tiny restaurant Po in Manhattan with not much more than optimism. Following a running start, he sold his stake.

But Batali's lusty take on traditional Italian fare first earned the media spotlight in 1998 at Babbo Ristorante e Enoteca, his Greenwich Village restaurant. There, the chef has seamlessly combined traditional Italian gastronomic principles with intelligent culinary adventure as a pivotal element in his empire. With a larger-than-life persona, he also blasted onto television screens, the exposure helping integrate his love of Italy's traditional cuisine into the way twenty-first century America eats, all the while establishing himself as the American king of Italian cooking.

The savvy chef likes being in public—whether on television, radio, or the Internet—to promote Italian food, his restaurants, and his cookware line. Batali readily acknowledges that he enjoys his celebrity status, but says that his objective is always to make people happy. Batali believes:

"IT SHOULD BE LOVE AND JOY, MUSIC, ART, DANCE, AND BEING TOGETHER THAT DRIVES US TO COOK, TO EAT, AND TO SHARE."

Batali's television appearances are many and varied, expressing the wide range of his interests and talents. He's hosted a variety of programs for the Food Network, including *Ciao America, Molto Mario,* and *Iron Chef America.* In the fall of 2008, Mario co-hosted a PBS series with Mark Bittman, Gwyneth Paltrow, and Spanish actress Claudia Bassols called *Spain . . . On the Road Again.*

The Mario brand continues to expand. Batali and partner Joe Bastianich now have fifteen restaurants in New York, Las Vegas, and Los Angeles, with more planned. The establishments are singular variations on Italian or Spanish themes, familiar territory for the partners. Eataly, the largest Italian food and wine marketplace in the world, opened in 2010 with multiple eating areas and a rooftop Italian beer garden. Batali and his partners also cultivate interests in vineyards and olive oil.

The Batali/Bastianich organization employs more than 1,500 people, all trained to achieve the level of skill and dedication required as a commitment to genuine hospitality. Batali has a heartfelt and ambitious goal: "I want to do the best job for our staff by making them happier and wealthier and for our customers, by satisfying them—making sure that everyone is constantly challenged, working together on every level of everything."

The strength of the operations is teamwork. Batali promotes from within and encourages the climb up. When Batali interviews talent, he's seeking something special. "I'm looking for the clarity in their eyes and a passionate commitment. I'm not looking for someone who's hoping to get a springboard to be the next TV chef. I can teach a monkey how to make linguine with clam sauce but I can't teach a monkey how to love the clam," Batali quips. Chefs, he says, should appreciate the variations that occur in a restaurant from month to month and they should look at their work "as a research project as opposed to just a construction job."

"The most outstanding award we ever received was Best New Restaurant for Babbo," Batali says about winning recognition from the James Beard Foundation in 1999. "It offers probably the single greatest message for inspiring young chefs. I'll never forget the elation, the feeling of contentment knowing that all of the work that we put into it got recognized.

Being in his restaurants is what Batali likes best. The New York location of Otto Enoteca Pizzeria is less than a block away from his home near Washington Square, and he rotates between nearby Babbo, Casa Mono (a Spanish-style taverna), Lupa (a Roman-style trattoria), Bar Jamon (a tapas bar), and Del Posto (a white-tablecloth Italian restaurant).

The chef's identity is unmistakable, partly because of his familiar face and ponytail, and partly due to his signature orange wardrobe, an ingredient in his multitiered marketing strategy. Orange was also the color his sons, Leo and Benno, wore as kids so they could be easily spotted among the other children on the playground. Hence, Batali has deemed orange the "Batali National Color" and he calls his outfits "Bitaly," a play on his name and heritage. From bright orange Crocs, which he runs through the dishwasher, to shorts as his daily attire, the color is ever present. He wears Crocs out of practicality. He says, "I mean come on. Crocs are the single most comfortable shoe. They get the fashion blogs really pissed off because apparently they don't like them. But I don't give a darn about it—I'm very comfortable, and they're very recognizable. People can sight you from a ways away."

The bag-of-doughnuts look is designed for comfort, not to impress. He'd like to wear fancy clothes, Batali confesses, but he just doesn't have the time or inclination to find them. Now that he's dressed himself in a signature style, he probably won't change. His fashion statement is as much an element of branding as his name or the Blood Orange Bellinis offered at Babbo.

CAVATELLI *with* PASTA ENRICO

PESTO

8 ounces fresh basil

1 cup roasted almonds

3 garlic cloves, peeled

1 ounce fresh mint, black or spearmint

Salt

9 ounces tomatoes, peeled and cut lengthwise into ½-inch slices

2 serrano chiles, seeded

1 teaspoon chili flakes

1 cup extra-virgin olive oil

Freshly ground black pepper

1 pound cavatelli, fresh or dried

⅔ cup toasted bread crumbs

Pecorino Siciliano

1. In a large pot, bring 6 quarts water and 2 tablespoons salt to a boil.

2. Meanwhile, make the pesto: In a mortar or a food processor, pound or process the basil, almonds, garlic, mint, and a pinch of salt until creamy. Reserve.

3. Separately pound or process the tomatoes, chiles, and chili flakes. Blend the tomatoes into the basil mixture, adding the oil and seasoning with salt and pepper. Put the pesto in a large serving bowl.

4. Add the pasta to the boiling water and cook until tender yet al dente, 6 to 8 minutes. Drain. Add the pasta to the serving bowl, tossing to coat. Garnish with the bread crumbs. Serve with Pecorino Siciliano grated at the table.

SERVES 4

GRILLED GUINEA HEN *with* FREGULA *and* BLACK TRUFFLE VINAIGRETTE

MARINADE

1 red onion, diced

½ cup balsamic vinegar

½ cup extra-virgin olive oil

¼ cup honey

2 tablespoons fresh thyme leaves

1 tablespoon freshly ground black pepper

8 guinea hen legs, deboned, with skin

VINAIGRETTE

1 cup sherry vinegar

1 cup ¼-inch shallot slices

1 tablespoon Dijon mustard

3 cups extra-virgin olive oil

1 cup finely chopped black truffles

Kosher salt

Freshly ground black pepper

FREGULA

1½ cups fregula pasta

2 ears corn, shucked

2 tablespoons extra-virgin olive oil

¾ cup chicken stock

¼ cup freshly grated
Parmigiano-Reggiano cheese

To make the marinade

1. In a 5-quart covered glass casserole, combine the onion, vinegar, oil, honey, thyme, and pepper. Put the guinea hen legs in the marinade, turning to coat on all sides. Cover and refrigerate for 8 hours or overnight.

To make the vinaigrette

1. In a 12-inch sauté pan over medium heat, add the vinegar and shallots and cook until the shallots are soft. Drain the shallots. In a food processor or blender, purée the shallots with the mustard. With the motor on high, drizzle the oil into the shallots and mustard until the mixture emulsifies. Whisk in the truffles. Season with salt and pepper. Reserve.

To make the fregula

1. Preheat the grill and prepare an ice water bath.

2. In a medium saucepan over high heat, bring 3 quarts water and salt to a boil. Add the pasta and cook until just tender, 10 to 12 minutes. Plunge the pasta into the ice water. Drain the pasta, dry well, and reserve.

3. Brush the corn ears with the oil, season with salt and pepper, and place them on the grill, turning every 2 minutes until all sides are nicely charred and the kernels are just beginning to burst. Remove the corn from the grill. When the ears are cool enough to handle, cut the kernels from the cobs with a sharp knife.

4. In a 12-inch sauté pan over high heat, combine the fregula, corn, and stock, bringing them to a boil. Continue boiling until the stock is absorbed into the grain, about 5 minutes. Add the Parmigiano-Reggiano, season with salt and pepper, and toss over high heat for 1 minute. Reserve.

5. Remove the guinea hen legs from the marinade and pat dry. Place them skin-side down over the hottest part of the grill until dark brown and crisp on the skin sides, 6 to 7 minutes. Season with salt and pepper. Turn and cook on the other sides until just cooked through, 4 to 5 minutes more. Keep warm.

6. Divide the fregula among four warmed dinner plates. Place two guinea hen legs on each plate, drizzle with the black truffle vinaigrette, and serve immediately.

SERVES 4

GRILLED LAMB HEART SPIEDINI *with* CARDOONS, POTATOES, *and* SWEET PEPPER VINAIGRETTE

LAMB HEARTS

1 cup extra-virgin olive oil

¼ cup vermentino or other dry white wine

1 bunch fresh mint, finely chopped

1 tablespoon chili flakes

4 lamb hearts, diced into 1-inch cubes

CARDOONS AND POTATOES

1 pound raw cardoons, peeled and cut into 3-inch pieces

2 medium, waxy potatoes (about 8 ounces)

Extra-virgin olive oil

1 lemon, juiced and zested

1 teaspoon chili flakes

VINAIGRETTE

1 red bell pepper

¼ cup red wine vinegar

3 tablespoons extra-virgin olive oil

1 tablespoon mustard seeds

1 tablespoon dried oregano

6 wooden skewers, soaked in water overnight

1 teaspoon fennel pollen

1. In a large bowl, combine the oil, wine, mint, and 1 tablespoon of the chili flakes. Add the lamb heart and marinate at least 30 minutes, preferably overnight.

2. Preheat a grill or plancha to high heat.

3. In a large saucepan, combine the cardoons, potatoes, and water to cover. Bring to a boil, until the cardoons and potatoes are tender, about 15 minutes. Strain and cool. Cut the cardoons into matchsticks. Dice the potatoes into ½-inch cubes. Reserve.

4. Roast the pepper over an open flame until blackened. Place it in a paper bag to rest for 5 minutes. Peel off the darkened skin and remove the seeds and stem. Place the pepper in a food processor or blender with the vinegar, oil, mustard seeds, and oregano. Process or blend until smooth. Season with salt and pepper. Reserve.

5. Toss the cardoons and potatoes with olive oil, the lemon juice and zest, and the chili flakes. Divide among six plates.

6. Place 3 pieces of lamb heart on each skewer. Grill the skewers until nicely charred, turning after 2 minutes. Place 1 skewer on each plate, drizzle with vinaigrette, and sprinkle lightly with fennel pollen. Serve immediately.

SERVES 6

AS ROMA	80
AC MILAN	70
SAMPDORIA	67
PALERMO	65
NAPOLI	59
JUVENTUS	55

2006

ALFRED PORTALE

CHAPTER *seventeen*

CHEF ALFRED PORTALE LOOKS AS IF HE STEPPED FROM A PAGE OF *GQ* MAGAZINE. WEARING A FITTED BLACK CHEF'S JACKET AND WELL-PRESSED DESIGNER JEANS, HE'S AS COSMOPOLITAN AS HIS RESTAURANT, GOTHAM BAR AND GRILL. He speaks quietly with staff, seeming to feel the dining room's rhythm, aware of everything around him. Expectations run high at Gotham Bar and Grill. His customers expect the pinnacle of a dining experience and Portale expects them to have it.

Almost three decades into the restaurant's success, it's still critical to him that the menu is creative, fresh, and contemporary and that the service remains well tuned. This persistent creativity makes Gotham feel like the city's hottest new place, even though it's long been a pillar of New York's dining favorites. One of three children, Alfred Portale grew up in Buffalo, New York. His father worked for the United States government. His mother was a homemaker and an early volunteer for the Meals On Wheels program. She sent her children to school with nourishing homemade lunches, which Portale swapped with other kids. "I just wanted Hostess Cupcakes," he laughs.

On Sunday afternoons, Portale and his siblings, parents, aunts, uncles, and cousins would gather for a gigantic Sunday dinner. The young Alfred helped in the kitchen. "It was important," he says. "It wasn't sophisticated, but it gave me an appreciation for cooking."

Drawing lessons and a well-developed color sense led Portale to designing jewelry—rings, engraved belt buckles, and gem-set hair combs. When all his samples were stolen at a trade show, he took it as an omen to look for another career. Portale had recently discovered the elaborate color photographs in Paul-Henri Pellaprat's *L'Art Culinaire Moderne*. The photographs inspired him to segue to a new career, from designing jewelry to the culinary arts. "There were photographs of cold buffets. Silver trays, spiny lobsters standing upright, little medallions and truffle cutouts and aspic spliced right up the tail. I thought it was like edible jewelry," he says. "And I thought: That's what I could do. I could apply my love of design to this."

Portale worked for two Buffalo restaurants as a prerequisite to enrollment at the Culinary Institute of America. He smiles. "I totally believed I could enroll at the Culinary Institute, graduate, and within two years, be out there creating elaborate buffets." He smiles again. "It was very different from what I imagined. When you're a youngster, you don't understand that this is a lifetime of study. I thought when I went to culinary school I graduate and instantly become a head chef."

Graduating at the top of his class in 1981, he spent his first six months postculinary school peeling potatoes in France. The more he learned about the rigors of being a chef, the more he loved the art and craft of preparing a dish. Portale was ready for much more.

When he returned to New York, he worked in French restaurants. "While the chefs of those restaurants were not my mentors, I did study them and read their cookbooks.

I READ COOKBOOKS CONSTANTLY. IT IS HOW MY CREATIVE PROCESS WORKS. IT'S LIKE DOING MENTAL CALISTHENICS,"

he says. Portale starts by reading the indexes and turns to the page of a dish that interests him and reads the ingredients, but he never looks at the directions. He explains, "I look at the flavor combinations, textures, and the inspiration for the dish."

Gotham was a struggling operation with a zero-star *New York Times* rating when Portale was hired in 1985 as the fourth chef during the restaurant's first year. It was a cavernous space. He revamped the kitchen, the menu, and the service. Barely six months later, the *New York Times* awarded the restaurant three stars.

When Portale joined the restaurant, the song "The Heat is On" became his anthem, the chef burning to make his mark. Portale wanted a restaurant that emulated the standards of the Michelin three-star restaurants in which he trained, but designed with his own buoyant twist. "Initially, I was interested in chefs who were cooking complex and highly technical French cuisine. That was very important to my development," he says. "Even today, the young chefs have to do their Ferran Adrià technique. They want to do something that nobody's ever done; the more technically complicated, the better. I think that's a young male chef's affliction.

I had it too, but I was tempered and influenced by the French chefs I worked under, legendary chefs such as Michel Guérard, the brothers Troisgros, and Jacques Maximin. They gave me an excellent appreciation for products and flavors and honesty in cooking. I applied their training to my design sense and developed my own personal style."

Noted food columnist and author John Mariani says that Portale became chef at Gotham as that particular New York–style restaurant was in its ascendency. Portale, thoroughly grounded in classic technique, gave New Yorkers sophisticated and refined cuisine, while also displaying his largesse, his exuberance, and his multilevel approach to flavors and textures. "His 'tower' dishes were not gimmickry. They were absolutely right for a vertical city with so much going on at every level," says Mariani.

Portale seems an unlikely rebel, but his work demonstrates otherwise. Given a free hand, he melded his classical French foundation with the California food revolution's outlook, breaking convention, building ingredients layer upon layer. The first act of rebellion from the young chef was his towering architectural plating— a style that resonated through the restaurant world.

Then Gotham became one of the first upscale restaurants to relax the formal dress code to business casual—a downtown kind of attitude. As a result, former *New York Times* restaurant critic Ruth Reichl declared, "You feel as comfortable in Gotham in jeans as you do in a tuxedo and are treated with the same warmth and respect by the staff either way."

When the chef, who had been used to working in three dimensions, arrived at Gotham, he didn't like the traditional flat look of plated food. He used his design aesthetic and art background to arrange ingredients as jewel-toned sculptures. The highly structured presentations were a product of his desire to create complex, labor-intensive, beautiful food, and to enhance flavors by starting with simple, clean combinations and punctuating them with beautiful, stylish presentations. Quickly emulated—sometimes successfully, other times not—his towering food regularly provoked the wrath of waiters everywhere, teetering through America's dining rooms, balancing food monoliths.

He remembers the comments. "People wondered how many chefs we had working in the kitchen and how were we creating this dynamic and complex food," he says. The answer is by building enough controls into each dish, by finding a place for everything, by deciding on exact specifications for size, shape, height, length, and depth, and by measuring to the millimeter—all to produce consistently fine food at high volume.

The plating style at Gotham has since evolved. Portale no longer assembles skyscrapers, but plating continues to be as meticulously designed as jewelry. It's a different balancing act now—one of multicultural flair. "The influences of various cuisines represent New York City and the energy of New York," he says, speaking as a pioneer of the "New American Cuisine" movement. With an emphasis on seasonality and local produce, he lets the ingredients speak for themselves. He calls it "clean cooking." Gotham has longstanding relationships with a variety of farmers and a steady source of fresh ingredients. The menu changes monthly in accordance with availability, although favorite dishes are rotated.

At Gotham, Portale trains a new generation of chefs who carry forward his techniques when they open their own restaurants. He believes young chefs can now find training opportunities in a number of American cities as an alternative to France. When Portale hires sous-chefs, he looks for passion and desire. He believes their time at Gotham should help them to grow, stay motivated, and be challenged. In the kitchen, he watches for cooks who have a respect for ingredients and a delicate touch. "Those are the people who ultimately do a great job," he says.

His first protégé was his first sous-chef, Tom Valenti, now executive chef and co-owner of Ouest. Jacinto Guadarrama has been at Gotham even longer than Portale, starting as a dishwasher, but Portale guided him to his current position, chef de cuisine. Bill Telepan, chef/owner of the eponymous Telepan, and Gotham alum, is not surprised that Gotham is still spectacular. "Alfred's attention to detail is still as evident as it was when I worked with him fifteen years ago," he says. "It is something I always reflect on. He is also someone who was always there to teach and listen. He encouraged me to develop skills that I use to this day." Chefs who have worked under him acknowledge that Portale allowed them to grow due to his management style—even-tempered, organized, good to be around, and reaching for the best without shortcuts. "He's a consummate professional," colleagues say. Even when chefs head to a bar, unwinding after the restaurant closes, Portale goes home.

Portale's empathy and tolerance for aspiring chefs is one of his greatest contributions. He remembers how hard it was when he was a Culinary Institute of America extern looking for a position with a good restaurant. Portale knows he was lucky to get one. He tries to pass that luck along. "We have a big crew in the kitchen. I encourage externs from the Culinary Institute and the local French Culinary Institute."

Tom Colicchio, who went on to make his own culinary name with Craft restaurants, left Gotham after only one week. Two years later, he was again working at Gotham and parking his motorcycle in the basement. But those were early days. Today it's unlikely motorcycles would be allowed in the basement. Now, at the top of a fulfilling career, Colicchio was named the 2010 James Beard Foundation Outstanding Chef. "We attract good people," says Portale. "It's no secret that a lot of great chefs come through here. When you're new in a profession, you need an environment like this, where you can really learn. It's intellectual, but it's also very physical."

Portale remembers when kitchens in French restaurants were "war zones," as he says. "I don't know about today, but when I was there, it was very tough. The older chefs would play tricks on you, turn off your stove, turn up the heat on your sauce and burn your stuff. They'd throw out your *mise en place*. The cooks would yell at the waiters and the waiters would yell at the cooks—it was a constant battle." As a result of that exposure, he feels strongly that the discipline is tough enough without adding to it. This attitude alone makes Portale different. "It's so distracting when there's yelling and screaming

and conflict," he says. He tries to eliminate all that from his restaurant. "Here we treat each other professionally and with respect."

Portale has watched the restaurant business evolve. "It's a quicker path to glory. Things happen faster. Cooks are better educated, better informed, and more aggressive. Chefs are treated like rock stars, or the television personalities they so often are," Portale reflects. He notes that the greatest TV chefs began as accomplished working chefs, pointing to Colicchio, Batali, Lagasse, Flay, Morimoto, and DiSpirito. Portale, who continues to have his share of the spotlight, says he admires "guys like Wolfgang Puck and Thomas Keller and Jean-Georges Vongerichten, these modern legends who work so hard," he says, shaking his head. "The amount of sacrifice required to run a restaurant like The French Laundry is extraordinary."

Until recently, Portale consciously refrained from expanding Gotham to multiple locations. He made a decision to be part of his children's lives. He limited his outside projects to writing cookbooks and consulting, collaborating on a renewal of the Philadelphia restaurant the Striped Bass in 2004. His three books are *Alfred Portale's Gotham Bar and Grill Cookbook* (1997), *Alfred Portale's Twelve Seasons Cookbook* (2000), and *Alfred Portale Simple Pleasures* (2004).

In October 2008, as one daughter finished college and his second daughter was beginning, Portale decided to finally expand, opening Gotham Steak to great success at the newly restored Fontainebleau Hotel in Miami. "Opening a restaurant takes a lot of time," he says. "Now the steak house is running really well. It has a great team, front and back of the house, and is very successful."

How does Portale relax? By building in an entirely different way: working with wood. He creates 1950s mid-century modern furniture—tables, desks, sideboards, and dressers for his home. "I love the Hamptons and the sound of the ocean," he says, "but my equipment is noisy and I was concerned about disturbing my neighbors. I've moved my woodworking shop to the Berkshires." Alfred Portale is considerate even when he relaxes.

BEET SALAD *with* MANGO, FETA, ORANGE, *and* MINT

2 large red and golden beets,
washed but not peeled

2 tablespoons olive oil

Coarse salt

Freshly ground black pepper

3 oranges, peeled and separated into segments

1/4 cup coarsely chopped fresh mint

1 tablespoon minced shallots

4 ounces Greek feta cheese, crumbled into
large pieces (approximately 1 cup)

1 ripe mango, cut into medium dice

Microgreens, for garnish (optional)

VINAIGRETTE

4 1/2 teaspoons extra-virgin olive oil

2 teaspoons balsamic vinegar

1 teaspoon freshly squeezed orange juice

1. Preheat the oven to 400°F.

2. In a bowl, toss the beets with the oil and season them with the salt and pepper. Put the beets on a roasting pan and cover them with foil. Roast in the oven until tender, about 1 1/2 hours. (They are done when a sharp, thin-bladed knife can easily pierce through to their center.) Remove the pan from the oven, remove the beets from the pan, and set them aside to cool.

3. While the beets are roasting, make the vinaigrette: In a small bowl, whisk together the oil, vinegar, and orange juice. Season with salt and pepper. Set aside.

4. When they are cool enough to handle, peel the beets and cut them into 1/2-inch dice. Put them in a bowl with 1 cup of the orange segments, the mint, and the shallots. Add the vinaigrette, season with salt and pepper, and toss gently.

5. Transfer the salad to a platter.

6. Arrange the cheese, mango dice, and the remaining orange sections on top. Garnish with microgreens, if desired, and serve.

SERVES 4

CURRY-SPICED MUSCOVY DUCK BREAST *with* FRAGRANT BASMATI RICE

DUCK

4 boneless Muscovy duck breasts with skin and wing attached (about 8 ounces each)

1 tablespoon spicy Madras curry powder

1 stalk lemongrass, thinly sliced

4 large shallots, thinly sliced

1 bunch fresh cilantro, roughly chopped

6 or 7 scallions, thinly cut into slices

6 garlic cloves, cut into slices

2 ounces fresh ginger, peeled and thinly sliced

4 pieces foie gras (2 ounces each)

APRICOT-CHERRY CHUTNEY

1/3 cup white vinegar

1 tablespoon chopped fresh ginger

1 large garlic clove, roughly chopped

1 1/2 cups dried apricots, cut into 1/2-inch-thick slices

1/2 cup dried sour cherries

1/2 cup golden raisins

3/4 cup plus 2 tablespoons sugar

1/4 teaspoon salt

Cayenne pepper

BASMATI RICE

2 cups basmati rice

6 tablespoon canola oil

2 tablespoons blanched, sliced cashews

1/2 cup finely chopped onion

1 cinnamon stick

1 cup milk

1/4 cup golden raisins

1/2 teaspoon ground cardamom

Salt

Freshly ground black pepper

1/4 cup chopped fresh cilantro

3 tablespoons yogurt

SAUCE

1 tablespoon canola oil

6 or 7 scallions, coarsely chopped

1/2 small onion, chopped

5 garlic cloves, roughly chopped

1 ounce fresh ginger, peeled and thinly sliced

1 teaspoon spicy Madras curry powder

2 cups brown chicken stock

1/4 cup white chicken stock

1 tablespoon unsalted butter

Freshly ground white pepper

GARNISHES

Yogurt

1/4 cup microgreens or 4 sprigs fresh cilantro

CONTINUED

To prepare the duck

1. Using a sharp knife, trim any excess skin from the duck breasts, and score the skin lightly in a crosshatch pattern; do not cut into the flesh. Remove and discard the wing tip, but leave the remaining two wing sections attached to the breast. Sprinkle the curry powder evenly on both sides of each duck breast. In a small bowl, combine the lemongrass, shallots, cilantro, scallions, garlic, and ginger. Sprinkle half of the marinade on the bottom of a baking dish, lay the duck breasts over the marinade, and sprinkle the other half of the marinade over them. Cover with plastic wrap and refrigerate for 24 hours.

To make the chutney

1. In a blender, combine the vinegar, ginger, and garlic and pulse until the mixture is almost smooth. Transfer to a nonreactive heavy-bottomed medium saucepan. Add the dried fruits, sugar, salt, and cayenne to taste, then pour in water to barely cover and stir well. Bring to a simmer over medium-low heat and cook, stirring frequently, until the chutney is thick and syrupy, 45 minutes to 1 hour. Let cool completely and reserve.

To make the rice

1. Put the rice in a colander and rinse under cold water for 2 to 3 minutes. Transfer the rice to a bowl, add 3 cups water, and let it soak for 30 minutes. Strain the rice from the water, saving the water. Set the rice and water aside.

2. In a medium saucepan, heat the oil over medium heat. Add the cashews and toast for 2 minutes, then remove the nuts from the pan and set aside. Add the onions to the pan and cook for 4 minutes, until softened. Add the cinnamon and cook for 2 minutes longer, until fragrant. Add the rice and cook, stirring for 5 to 6 minutes, until it just begins to brown. Add the milk, raisins, cardamom, and reserved soaking water. Season with salt and pepper.

3. Bring the rice to a boil over high heat, reduce the heat to medium, cover, and simmer for about 10 minutes. Reduce the heat and steam for 10 minutes longer—let the rice rest for 5 minutes, and reserve warm. Stir in the reserved cashews, cilantro, and yogurt before serving.

To make the sauce

1. In a saucepan, heat the oil over medium heat. Add the scallions, onion, garlic, and ginger and cook for 3 to 4 minutes. Add the curry powder and cook for approximately 1 minute. Add the stocks, bring to a boil, reduce the heat, and simmer for 15 minutes. Remove from the heat, stir in the butter to enrich the sauce, season with the pepper, and reserve.

2. Remove the duck breasts from the refrigerator, wipe off the marinade, and let them come to room temperature. Season with salt and pepper, then place the duck breasts skin-side down in a large cold sauté pan. Cook the breasts over medium heat for about 10 minutes, until nicely browned. Turn and cook the second sides for 2 to 3 minutes longer, until medium rare. Remove from the pan and let rest for 10 minutes. While the duck breasts are resting, sear the foie gras in the same pan and cook until warm in the center, 2 to 3 minutes.

To serve

1. Spoon yogurt onto each plate. Using a fork, fluff the rice, and arrange some on each plate using a ring mold. Remove the wing bones from the duck breasts and french the ends. Slice the duck breast and fan it beside the rice. Arrange the frenched wings beside the slices. Place the foie gras on top of the duck breast, top with a spoonful of chutney, and spoon sauce over. Garnish with the microgreens and serve.

SERVES 4

2007

MICHEL RICHARD

CHAPTER *eighteen*

CHEF MICHEL RICHARD APPROACHES FOOD AS A FINE ARTIST, A CALLING HE FLIRTED WITH AS A YOUNG MAN. Where some chefs may simply see vegetables, Richard envisions a mosaic of contrasting hues, textures, and forms. His innate creativity jumps from palette to palate. In what he considers his flagship eatery, Michel Richard Citronelle in Washington, D.C., guests seated around the chef's table in a glass-enclosed kitchen can witness art being made at the stoves.

Richard's artistry is displayed in the dishes he creates as well as his restaurant decor. In Citronelle, his edible works are served in the dining room, and one of his drawings is modestly displayed. The rotund chef, who paints at night, cares little if his quirky imagination is working either with a whisk or a brush. In his mind, they're interchangeable. He does care that patrons leave his restaurants fulfilled and enthusiastic about a series of delightfully colored dishes brimming with an array of flavors.

Richard is a superior technician. Serious, intense, and focused, he understands how ingredients can be manipulated in unconventional ways to realize his artistic vision. Yet he's also a chef with a droll culinary edge. His trompe l'oeil presentations often elicit laughter from diners. His fundamental joy in his craft is displayed in both his food and his personality. Richard is all about creating delectable surprises.

Russ Parsons, food writer for the *Los Angeles Times*, a former cook under Richard, and member of the James Beard Foundation's Who's Who of Food & Beverage, calls some of Richard's dishes at Citronelle "splendid goofs."

A celebrated menu item at Citronelle appears to be traditional fettuccine. But once tasted, the diner discovers it is sautéed onion strips rather than pasta. With a culinary sleight of hand, Richard infuses such dishes with a sense of humor and sends infectious wonderment to the table. Michel Richard Citronelle, which opened in 1994 at Georgetown's Latham Hotel, is as fresh and bright as the cuisine served there. Quirky touches, such as a fluid, ever-changing, colorful "mood wall," are appropriate for an adventurous chef who embodies the spirit of joie de vivre.

Born in 1948 in Brittany, in northwestern France, Richard had a hardscrabble childhood while his mother worked as the family's sole support. Michel became the household chef at eight years old. "I was responsible for the food for my brothers and sisters," says the oldest of five children. "I was their five-star restaurant. I cooked, and was enjoying myself!"

Richard really fell in love with food for the first time, though, at nine or ten years old during an Easter vacation spent with a schoolmate whose father owned a restaurant. "When I entered the kitchen, it was for me paradise. The pastry chef let me help make a little tart. I fell in love with it all," Richard remembers. He fell hard. He adored the white hats, aprons, the abundance of food, and most of all, the beautiful patrons he saw having a good time in the dining room. It became a burning, passionate affair.

Richard endured a harsh apprenticeship at a pâtisserie in Reims, France, at fourteen, learning the unforgiving techniques of making pastry under an often brutally demanding chef. But that was the nature of a circa-1960s French apprenticeship. Three years later, he moved to Paris, thrived under stimulus and encouragement, and rose to the top position at celebrated pastry chef Gaston Lenôtre's fashionable pâtisserie. Lenôtre was Richard's guardian angel, and Richard's third book, *Sweet Magic* (2010) is dedicated to Lenôtre, who died in 2009. It features original art by Richard to illustrate the recipes.

In 1974, Lenôtre sent his protégé to open a pâtisserie in Manhattan. Armed with a two-hour lesson in the English language, twenty-six-year-old Richard made his way across the Atlantic. The Brittany native fell in love once again. "I was enchanted. I felt so small in France," he recalls. "I felt like a big deal in America. I felt like anything was possible."

Lenôtre's New York venture closed quickly because, as Richard remembers, in 1975 there was no dessert culture in America. But he loved the United States and he loved his work, so he stayed. "You don't leave a girlfriend when you are in love," he says. "I saw this country would be nice to me." So Richard headed west.

During his drive across the country that ended at a small pastry shop in Santa Fe, he found a roadside Kentucky Fried Chicken restaurant, and with it, a revelation. "It was so delicious: moist inside, and crunchy outside. In France, we don't have a lot of crunchy food. I discovered texture in this country. Crunch, crunch, crunch. In France, I thought the food was boring, boring, boring. French chef, French vegetables, French people, and French food," he says. He's tickled that some people call him "Captain Crunch."

Attracted by bright lights and stars, he moved on to Los Angeles, and opened the Michel Richard Pastry Shop in 1977, quickly gaining a reputation for having the city's premiere pastries. That might have been a happy enough ending to his story, but, after a few years there, Richard was unfulfilled. "I was thirty-five and tired of baking," he says. "I was losing part of myself."

When Paul Bocuse and Roger Vergé were in town to prepare a special event and heard there was a Lenôtre-trained pastry chef in Los Angeles, they asked Richard to make the dessert. That was followed by an invitation from Bocuse and Vergé to visit them in France. Richard accepted and there they encouraged him to make a monumental career change. His enthusiasm was rekindled and he determined to join their ranks as a great chef. "My dream was to become a chef, and my mother had told me to be a great chef I should learn to be a pastry chef first. But she didn't tell me how long I should wait before becoming a real chef. It only took me twenty-one years to do it," Richard explains.

"From these two great chefs, I learned when the food leaves the kitchen it goes to guests. When I worked in a pastry shop people come to pick up the dessert and take it home. You don't know what happens to it when it leaves the shop, and you don't get to watch people enjoy it. As a chef, you get to take care of the entire evening—not only the pastry, but the flowers, the smell of the room, the beautiful plates. You create the whole cornucopia of foods from savory to sweet."

He discovered from Bocuse and Vergé the importance of beauty and cleanliness in their restaurants, the magic of entertainment, the sophistication and synchronicity of the waiters, the feel of the tablecloths. Richard was impressed with the encompassing feel of perfect harmony.

As fashions and styles change, so, too, would Richard. His pâtisserie became his classroom, where he taught himself the other side of the kitchen, moving from his knowledge of sweets to tricky savory dishes, bringing along his flair for gorgeous plating and adornment. The lack of a traditional apprenticeship proved an asset in many respects: He did what he knew, and in his own way. Flavors and textures became his new layers.

Richard's style of food wizardry is rarely seen in a restaurant kitchen. From nouvelle cuisine's influence, he works to make food lighter than traditional French cooking. He borrows a little from here, and a little from there, using his curiosity and observations to highlight the results.

However, the man so in love with food has been fighting a lifelong battle with his own weight. Richard jokes without hesitation that his dream is to slim down. "I would love to be skinny," he says, smiling. "The doctor is telling me, and my wife is telling me, to be skinny. I want to please my doctor, and I want to please my wife, but I want to please myself. It is tough to be so happy with food.

I LOVE TO EAT. I LOVE GOOD FOOD. I LOVE HOW IT TASTES."

"I like to add little things to my dishes. Just a little salt. I love that so much. But some people don't like it. That's because they cook without salt," he says. Sometimes a guest will come into the restaurant and ask for salt-free food. "Soon people are going to ask us to cook with no seasoning at all. Or maybe just want a salad. Maybe then we could all be skinny. Maybe I should change the name of the restaurant to Hospital!" he laughs.

But the chef who adores good butter, and adds salt to his dishes, is adapting to the trends of healthier lifestyles and eating. He uses vegetable waters and juices to lighten his recipes. Cubes of pureed vegetables, fruit juices, and even mushroom jus are frozen. Later the cubes can be used to make sauces.

He admits, "It's fun. It's always a challenge. We need to learn the new style of eating." After all, he says, it is possible to have a salad and a carrot stick and make them both appealing and appetizing. "You can have your salad, and keep your carrot happy in the salad. Shredded carrot salad!"

Richard sees his job as creating surprising food—the food you don't eat every day. With the rise of the food culture, top chefs are willing to shell out whatever it takes for superior ingredients. Chefs also know that if they want to hold on to their customers, they have to be constantly coming up with new and imaginative menu items.

Richard is amazed at the variety of foods he is able to find in America. "In France when you go to a market, you only have a French market. Here we have such a variety! We have all of the Asian markets, Latino products . . . you go around the corner, and you find food everywhere. It's a potpourri. It's fabulous, just great," he enthuses.

While Richard has been an inspiration to chefs around the world, he has had his own culinary heroes. One of them was the late Jean-Louis Palladin, also an honored James Beard chef.

Ariane Daguin, the owner of D'Artagnan, a purveyor of such products as game birds and foie gras, met Richard through their mutual close friend, Palladin. "Jean-Louis told me you have to go see that crazy pastry chef over there," she recalls. "He was doing very avant-garde things. . . . Michel was combining hot and cold in a way nobody else was doing back then. He was looking at the other guys, and saying, 'Hey, I'm a chef, too.' You could tell he wanted to dazzle them." Palladin and Richard became the best of friends, each with a raucous sense of humor.

Beginning in 1987, Richard opened restaurants in Los Angeles, San Francisco, Baltimore, Santa Barbara, and Philadelphia, but they all eventually closed. He finally settled down at Michel Richard Citronelle in Washington, D.C., in 1994, and another in Carmel, California.

Then he did it again in 2004, opening the wildly successful Central Michel Richard, also based in Washington. "It was always my dream to have an American restaurant," he says. The more casual bistro-style Central was awarded the 2008 James Beard Best New Restaurant, and is a rollicking scene as vibrant as the nation's capital. Central's logo is even a self-portrait cartoon doodled by Richard.

At Citronelle, guests witness a dedicated, focused crew under the watchful eye of one of the world's most acclaimed chefs. Richard is not a celebrity chef too busy for his first love, the kitchen. He gives orders and dips spoons to taste sauces. He feels very strongly about the people working with him. "I love them," he says about his staff. "I always feel like there are not bad employees, only bad leaders. You have to take what you know and you have to train them, teach them. You have to coach them standing right next to them." And that feeling explains why the chef with a sense of humor spends so much of his time in the kitchen.

In 2006, the chef, who lists "reading old cookbooks" as his only real hobby, published his second cookbook, *Happy in the Kitchen*, a light-hearted, sometimes whimsical approach to gourmet cooking at home. Home is where his heart is full.

Looking back at over forty years in professional kitchens, Richard has few regrets. He's respected. Love is returned. His friends are close. Celebrities, stars, and world leaders dine with him. President and Mrs. Obama chose Citronelle for their first date-night dinner after they moved into the White House. (He had the 72-hour short ribs; she had the lobster burger.)

"Some people ask me 'Are you going to retire?' It is just fabulous. I have so much to do I cannot retire. I cannot stop. I've been having fun. It has been a nice voyage, a nice trip with cooking," Richard muses. The past fifteen years particularly have been a great time, he says. "I feel like I'm a piece of food God created. There is nothing else I can do. Maybe painting. Maybe in a few years maybe you'll go to a modern art museum and see a Michel Richard painting," he says through a hearty laugh. "But probably not."

Instead, Richard recently designed a French menu for the café at the National Gallery of Art—a fitting place to serve the food of a culinary artist.

ONION FETTUCCINE *with* PARMESAN CHEESE

3 large yellow onions (about 2¼ pounds)

½ cup heavy cream, divided

1 large egg yolk

2 tablespoons unsalted butter

Fine sea salt

Freshly ground black pepper

2 tablespoons freshly grated Parmesan cheese, plus shaved Parmesan for garnish

Minced fresh chives, for garnish

1. Cut off the tops from the onions and peel the onions. Stand each onion on its cut end and, with a paring knife, cut one lengthwise slit from top to bottom, reaching just to the core. Cut the onions crosswise into ¹/8-inch slices with a sharp knife. You will have rings with open ends.

2. Separate the onions into strands, making about 8 cups loosely packed. Reserve the shorter strands for another use.

3. Fill a medium pot three-quarters full with water and bring it to a rolling boil. Reduce the heat to a simmer. Place a steamer basket in the pot over simmering water. Place the onion strands in the basket, cover, and steam for 5 to 6 minutes, until they are translucent but still "al dente." Remove the basket from the heat. The strands may be prepared several hours in advance.

4. In a small bowl, mix ¹/4 cup of the cream and the egg yolk. Set aside.

5. In a 12-inch sauté pan over medium heat, melt the butter. Add the remaining ¹/4 cup cream and simmer for 30 seconds.

6. Toss the onion strands with salt and pepper. Add the onions to the pan, cooking for 2 to 3 minutes, or until hot. Remove the pan from the heat and stir in the cream mixture and Parmesan. Adjust seasonings as needed.

7. With tongs, remove a portion of onions, letting excess sauce drip into the pan. Put the portion on a serving plate, arranging it in a small mound. Garnish with shaved Parmesan and chives and serve.

SERVES 4

_Duck_ SHABU SHABU

2 boneless, skinless duck breasts

1 cup shelled peas

1 cup thinly sliced asparagus

1 cup pearl onions, peeled and sliced

1 cup baby carrots, thinly sliced

1 cup thickly julienned turnip

1 cup thickly julienned rutabaga

MUSHROOM BROTH

3 pounds button mushrooms

4 shallots, thinly sliced

2 cups red wine

Salt

Freshly ground black pepper

1. Cover the duck breasts with plastic wrap and place them in the freezer for 1 hour, until partially frozen. Remove the plastic wrap. With a sharp knife, cut the breasts crosswise into paper-thin slices. Arrange them in a thin layer in the bottom of heatproof serving bowls, the slices just touching.

2. Prepare an ice bath by filling a 2-quart bowl three-quarters full of ice. Add cold water to the top of the ice.

3. Fill a medium saucepan with water and bring it to a rolling boil. Working with one type of vegetable at a time, blanch the peas, asparagus, onions, carrots, turnips, and rutabagas in the boiling water until just tender. Remove with a slotted spoon and plunge the vegetables into the ice bath to stop the cooking process. Drain and dry the vegetables before blanching the next batch.

4. Preheat the oven to 300°F.

To make the mushroom broth

1. Puree the mushrooms in a food processor. In a medium saucepan, combine the shallots and wine. Bring them to a boil and reduce by half. Add the mushroom puree and simmer over low heat for 20 minutes. Pass the mixture through a fine strainer, reserving mushroom solids for another use, if desired. Season with salt and pepper.

2. Evenly distribute the vegetables in the bowls on top of the duck.

3. Bring the broth to a boil.

4. When ready to serve, place the bowls in the oven for 4 minutes, until the duck is warm but not cooked. Serve immediately, pouring hot broth into bowls at the table.

SERVES 6

2008

GRANT ACHATZ

CHAPTER *nineteen*

WHEN TONGUE CANCER ROBBED GRANT ACHATZ OF HIS TASTE FOR MORE THAN A YEAR, IT DIDN'T STOP THE CHEF FROM REACHING AN EXALTED PINNACLE. On the night of June 8, 2008, when he accepted the James Beard Foundation Award for America's Outstanding Chef, Achatz told the audience that he used the discipline that served his young culinary career to survive the diagnosis. "What I didn't know at the time," Achatz said, "is that tenacity, that drive that I took in—would save my life." Some elements of his professional life were changed, he says, "but the general direction of where I was going before I was diagnosed is exactly where I would be now had I never had it."

Throughout his ordeal, the slim, quickly moving chef continued to work in his restaurant kitchen, meshing his sense of smell with his crew's sense of taste. His flavor memories and ferocious creativity bridged the gap. The experience did not define him as a chef, but gave him insight into his character. "I have a very strong belief that people needed to be aware of my fight with cancer. Because something I learned during that process was determination which could benefit a lot of people, not just people with cancer but sickness in general. So that's why I was so public with it."

Achatz's determination was apparent early on. His parents and other relatives operated a number of restaurants in Michigan, and he grew up in restaurant kitchens. From the time of his adolescence, he says, his life "has been devoted to tasting and memorizing flavors." Soon after enrolling at the Culinary Institute of America in 1993, straight out of high school, Achatz discovered that "food can be kind of an artistic medium versus just feeding people." He was determined to find work in a top American restaurant. He signed on with Charlie Trotter in Chicago but left after three months.

Following that experience, he spent the next three months eating in France, Italy, and England. "I thought about the food. I was absorbed in it," he remembers. Achatz then set his career goal of becoming the best. This meant learning from the best.

He sent a letter every day for a week in 1996 to Thomas Keller. The letters caught the chef's attention and on a Sunday, Keller telephoned Achatz out of curiosity. All he wanted was a job, a chance at his dreams, Achatz explained. Keller invited him for a two-day trial and after the second evening, made an offer.

Achatz had no idea what the job paid. He had no idea what the position would be. He didn't care. But his determination paid off with four rewarding years in the kitchen at The French Laundry in California. "Integrity and generosity were Keller's keys to success," says Achatz. "I don't want to be known for less than excellent. That's what integrity is to me." The two men connected, one leading and the other eagerly following.

Keller later arranged a brief *stage* for Achatz at El Bulli, where he observed the principles of chef Ferran Adrià's molecular gastronomy. As Achatz says, "Keller knew me well enough to recognize that this expression of creativity was what I was really interested in. First, there were inherent boundaries for what we created at The French Laundry just because of the concept. It is modern French food. So you couldn't really stray too far off that. And I was always trying to wiggle outside of the boundaries of those confines. I was kind of known for that. So he recognized it."

The El Bulli stage proved to be a pivotal point in Achatz's career. "It led me to realize that it was time to move on, because as amazing as my time was working for Keller, I was getting restless creating under his umbrella, and it was time to do something else." In 2001, Achatz left The French Laundry to become executive chef at the Chicago restaurant Trio, where he earned five stars from the Mobil Travel Guide in 2004. He began focusing intently on the bold culinary style that, four years later, would reach maturity at Alinea, and almost immediately assure his place in the culinary world.

Opening Alinea in 2005 with his business partner and closest friend, Nick Kokonas, was the achievement of a lifelong goal. When he met with the staff two days before opening, it was the first time the entire staff had gotten together. "Some of us had never even seen each other before," Achatz remembers. "Fifty of us gathered and I gave the welcome and opening speech. And, I said, 'We are about to open the best restaurant in the country, and anything less is simply not acceptable.' To even consider it not working, or people not accepting what you believed so wholeheartedly, was scary. It was a personal achievement. It wasn't an ego thing—it was more a very important thing to accomplish, but I knew that regardless, I achieved one of my life goals, which was very satisfying. I was scared to death. We put so much into Alinea. I said that we were going to do this and then, holy cow we did it!" In short time, Alinea has found a place among the most sought-after dining destinations in the world.

Achatz asks guests at Alinea for trust when they enter the private, unmarked door of the Chicago restaurant. Dining approaches performance art there. Each course is designed to astonish and provoke thought. Bits of food arrive suspended from wire or ingeniously crafted edible threads. Other courses are cradled within vertical rods, or brought out on tiny porcelain pedestals arranged in a row.

Black-clad servers pace the meal with almost clockwork precision. One dish may be presented with the admonition, "This is the centerpiece. Don't touch this with your hands." Food colors seem to brighten and deepen against the restaurant's expanses of gray, silver, and black. Making your way through the twenty-plus course Tour menu typically takes three luxurious hours. Everything coheres, and everything is carefully designed to showcase Achatz's creativity. He calls the style "progressive American" when people ask him to describe it. "I shy away from the term 'molecular gastronomy' because I don't think it's a fit description of what we do," clarifies Achatz.

No label could describe the range and avant-garde originality of his menus. Dining at Alinea requires imagination and a heart open to joyous delight. It's an all-encompassing experience, crafted to engage all the senses.

The restaurant embodies the fascination Achatz developed in California and Spain with new culinary techniques. Alinea quickly became a proving ground for his fast-growing repertoire, a place where he and his crew could cook whatever they liked and toss out the clunkers. This led to menus driven by inspirations and flavor combinations that proved to be as exciting as they were audacious.

It's not surprising that the restaurant's kitchen, with its induction burners, nitrous siphons, dehydrators, vacuum sealers, and sous-vide baths, has the aspect of a laboratory. Achatz is fastidious about his kitchen and equipment; floors are carpeted and vacuumed constantly. Stainless-steel workstations are smoothed free of scratches and dings, providing a pristine canvas upon which to work. His focus on unique combinations of texture and temperature has even inspired the invention of a new appliance, the AntiGriddle. It was developed in collaboration with an Illinois company called PolyScience that specializes in constant temperature control. The AntiGriddle can create, among other things, frozen foods with crunchy surfaces and creamy interiors. Achatz and his team continue to work with PolyScience on other intriguing ideas.

Like a good many of his freethinking colleagues, Achatz uses these instruments to manipulate tastes, aromas, and textures to create totally original combinations. He is also known for using starkly contrasting flavors in a single dish—such as duck, chocolate, blueberry, and Thai pepper.

But it's not all about innovation, edginess, and science. Achatz also relies on his classical cooking background to deliver the intended gastronomic effect. He says: "It's about crafting an experience, whether that's whipping hollandaise that we are going to serve or doing some crazy dehydration/freeze-running techniques. The way we blend it all together is not about trying to show science. There are some restaurants that try to do that—that's fine if it's what they want to do."

"WE'RE TRYING TO BREAK THE MONOTONY OF NOT ONLY FOOD TECHNIQUE, PRESENTATION, AND PREPARATION, BUT THE EMOTIONAL RESPONSE THAT YOU HAVE," ACHATZ SAYS. "IF WE CAN MAKE IT MORE INTERACTIVE, OR MORE ENTERTAINING, OR MAKE IT INTIMIDATING, OR MAKE IT FUN— THEN WE CREATE SOMETHING THAT'S NOT JUST ABOUT EATING AND FILLING YOUR STOMACH. IT'S AN EVENT."

Like a painter who sees shades of color that others do not, Achatz's creativity with food comes from a natural and keen sense of observation. As he puts it, "Everything inspires me. I think being creative, to me, is about being very aware of your surroundings and being very aware of what's going on in the world. An organic farmer from Michigan could bring a case of beautiful produce, and that might inspire a dish. It's completely unpredictable. I might be visiting an art gallery and see a particular texture or a particular form." Achatz could be outdoors on a sunny afternoon, watching his two sons play soccer with childlike enthusiasm, and that stirs a notion. "It's endless. It just comes from everywhere. There's no real template or documented way."

He thinks through new culinary ideas late at night in the empty restaurant by sketching various concepts. He then transfers the drawings to posters for the kitchen wall, so his staff can consider the concept. One bore the words "Capture spring. What is it? New, Fresh, Ice. Sprouts. Delicate. Gradual." The practice stimulates feedback and collaboration.

But the appeal of Achatz's food goes beyond the eye and the palate. It also takes aim at the intellect and even the diner's sense of nostalgia. With some of his flavors and aromas, Achatz tries to connect with the guest's memory bank. In this instance, he once said, the goal is to "transport people back to other times in their lives. It might happen with the scent created by pouring very hot water onto hyacinth blossoms, or placing a partly burned oak leaf alongside a serving of pheasant."

Then he takes his food fantasies a little farther by inventing thought-provoking ways to serve his creations. Achatz and designer/sculptor Martin Kastner collaborate to design Alinea's unique culinary assemblages—yet another expression of the chef's artistic side. Achatz realized that evolution in cooking was not accompanied by evolution in tableware, and sought to encourage it.

Kastner works with metals, wire, and glass to craft implements for Alinea that are functional as well as beautiful. They're essentially tabletop sculpture—adornment for gastronomy. As Achatz is taking new looks at cuisine, Kastner's creativity and zest are cutting new swaths through other traditions.

In the five short years since Alinea opened, Achatz and Nick Kokonas have proven their abilities. *Alinea*, their 2008 book, stunned the publishing industry with its remarkable production values. They launched it with an extensive, multitiered marketing platform that includes an interactive Web site. Further, they tapped into social media. Achatz is an active blogger and keeps a laptop by his side. Their second book, *Life, on the Line* followed in 2011.

Despite their monumental achievements, Achatz and Kokonas couldn't stand hearing people ask, "What's next?" They really didn't want to stop at Alinea's success. They had brought together such a unique and creative team that they wanted to expand on new ideas. Working again with Crucial Detail designer Martin Kastner, architect Steve Rugo, and interior designer Tom Stringer, their new projects are Next and The Aviary, which will be side by side at the Fulton Street Market in Chicago.

Next explores world cuisine, drawing from great moments in culinary history—or the future. "We want to take diners on a journey to the foods we find exciting, delicious, and important," says Achatz. "Our goal each season is to present the best possible menu from each culinary inspiration." There will be four menus a year, exhaustively researched and tested.

The Aviary next door is not exactly a bar or a lounge. There are no traditional bartenders, as chefs produce innovative and beautiful drinks paired with food. "Every great drink deserves a food pairing. We craft bites to pair with the drinks, much like we normally find drinks to pair with our bites," explains Kokonas "But here, there's no reservation or ticket, just walk right into the drink kitchen for an alcoholic tasting menu."

As Achatz puts it, "People ask me all the time, 'Well, when are you going to settle down? When are you going to retire?' And I'm, like, 'Retire? I'm thirty-six years old, man!' And that's the weird part about this. I've been so lucky to ascend at such a rapid pace so early in my life."

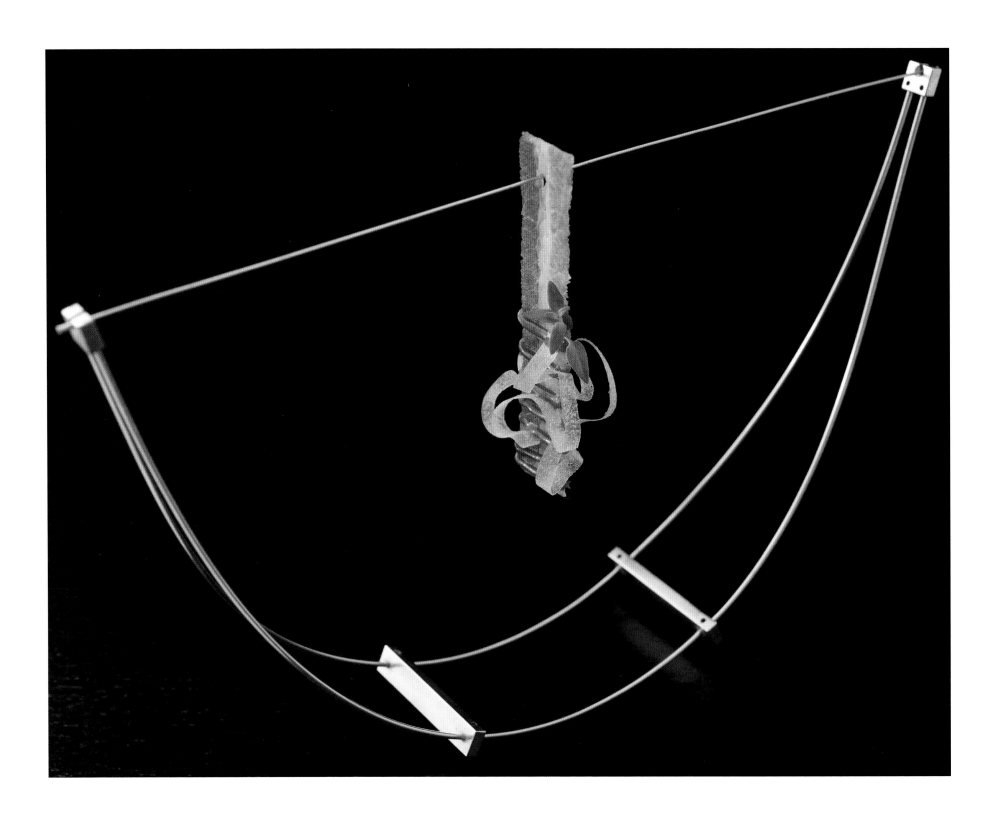

BACON, BUTTERSCOTCH, APPLE, THYME

8 strips bacon, 1/16 in/2 mm thick and 4 in/10 cm long

8¾ oz/250 g sugar
5¼ oz/150 g light corn syrup
13¼ oz/375 g heavy cream

2 Granny Smiths apples, halved and cored

Nonstick cooking spray

Freshly ground black pepper

8 tips young, fresh thyme, ½ in/12 mm long

1. Place the bacon on dehydrator trays and dehydrate at 170°F for 3 hours, or until dried and crisp. Reserve in an airtight container.

2. Line a baking sheet with a silicone mat. In a medium, heavy saucepan, heat the sugar and corn syrup over medium heat to 350°F. Slowly whisk in the cream and heat to 240°F. Pour onto the prepared baking sheet and let cool. Transfer the butterscotch to a pastry bag fitted with a small, round tip.

3. Preheat the oven to 375°F. Line a baking sheet with a silicone mat. Place the apples, cut-side down, on the prepared sheet. Roast for 30 minutes, or until very soft. Let cool on the tray. Scoop the flesh from the apple halves into a small bowl and discard peels. Transfer the flesh to a blender and blend until smooth. Strain through a *chinois* into a medium bowl.

4. Spray two 16-by-20-inch acetate sheets with nonstick cooking spray and wipe off the excess with a paper towel. Using a palette knife or offset spatula, evenly spread the apple puree on each sheet 1/16 in/2 mm thick. Transfer the sheets to dehydrator trays and dehydrate at 160°F for 45 minutes, or until they are the texture of fruit leather and can be peeled away. Cut into strips 1/8 in/3 mm wide and 4 in/10 cm long.

To assemble and serve

1. Gently hold a piece of bacon in one hand. Pipe butterscotch onto one half of the bacon, winding it around the slice and spacing the butterscotch lines 1/4 in/6 mm apart. Wind 6 apple ribbons around the bacon, using the butterscotch as glue and producing an organic looping look. Season the bacon with pepper. Attach the thyme to the bacon with a small amount of butterscotch. Suspend each bacon strip from a stainless-steel bow. Repeat with the remaining bacon slices.

SERVES 8

HOT POTATO, COLD POTATO, BLACK TRUFFLE, PARMESAN

3½ oz/100 g Yukon Gold potato, plus
1 medium Yukon Gold potato, unpeeled

8 oz/225 g black truffle juice

1 lb 2 oz/500 g heavy cream

1 oz/25 g white truffle oil

¼ oz/5 g kosher salt

15¾ oz/450 g clarified butter

1 oz/30 g butter, very cold

1 oz/30 g Parmesan cheese

3 fresh chives

2 fresh Perigord black truffles

Maldon sea salt

1. Peel the potato and cut it into ½-in/12-mm dice. In a medium saucepan, bring the potato and truffle juice to a boil over high heat. Reduce the heat to a simmer and cook for about 20 minutes, or until the potato is tender. Add the cream, return to a simmer, and remove from the heat.

2. Transfer to a blender and blend until smooth. With the blender running on high speed, add the truffle oil in a thin, steady stream. Add the salt and blend briefly. Strain through a *chinois* into a covered container. Refrigerate the potato soup for at least 8 hours.

3. Using a ½-in/12-mm parisienne scoop, scoop out spheres of potato flesh (you will need 8 spheres). In a small saucepan, cook the potato spheres in the clarified butter over medium heat for 20 minutes, or until tender. The butter will bubble, but the spheres should not brown. Remove from the heat and set aside until needed.

4. Cut the butter into eight ⅛-in/3-mm cubes, dipping a knife in hot water and wiping it dry before each cut. Freeze until needed.

5. Cut the Parmesan into eight small chunks, each about ⅛ in/3 mm wide.

6. Cut the chives on the bias into eight ½-in/12-mm lengths.

7. Using a mandoline or truffle slicer, cut the truffles to yield 8 very thin slices.

To assemble and serve

1. Pierce the side of each of eight paraffin bowls with a long stainless-steel pin. Slide 1 Parmesan chunk, 1 butter cube, and 1 chive length onto the pin, spacing them about ¼ in/6 mm apart. Fill the paraffin bowl about halfway with potato soup. Refrigerate the bowls. Gently reheat the potato spheres in the clarified butter. Remove the soup-filled bowls from the refrigerator. Slide 1 hot potato sphere onto each pin and drape the sphere with 1 truffle slice. Top each truffle slice with a few salt flakes.

SERVES 8

2009

DAN BARBER

CHAPTER *twenty*

ERUDITE, THOUGHTFUL, AND POLITICALLY WELL INFORMED, DAN BARBER IS THE VOICE OF A NEW GENERATION OF CHEFS IN THE FARM-TO-TABLE MOVEMENT. But he's really more dirt-to-roots-to-table than anything else.

Barber refutes labels, saying he has been doing all along what other chefs embarked upon twenty-five to thirty years ago. That was a critical movement, he acknowledges, but, with the proliferation of farmers' markets across America, that is "old news today." With the locavore movement as his foundation, Barber is taking the farm-to-table movement to a new level, hammering home the message that chefs must become more involved in raising awareness about the need to work with farmers to improve the quality, nutrition, and flavor of foods. Barber calls it the "recipe of agriculture." Barber grew up in New York City, but the happiest days of his youth were spent during summers with his brother and sister at Blue Hill Farm, his grandmother's 300-acre farm in the Berkshires of Massachusetts.

His grandmother was devoted to preserving the landscape. And in retrospect, Barber sees his childhood experience on her farm as having a strong influence on his decision to become a chef, "especially in the choice of what kind of chef I wanted to become," he notes. He points to that experience as having set him on the path that led him and his brother David, along with David's wife Laureen, to open Blue Hill restaurant in Greenwich Village in 2000, where Barber cooks food harvested from farms that have the same respect for agriculture, gastronomy, and preservation that his grandmother did.

But there were other important influences that led Barber to his culinary fate. He received a degree in English and political science from Tufts University in 1992, but he also took some courses in agriculture there that reignited an interest that he'd had since childhood. He read Wendell Berry, Rachel Carson, and other authors who wrote about agricultural and environmental issues, stimulating his interest in political connections to the food Americans eat.

After receiving his degree, Barber planned to take a scholarship in political science, but before the program even started, it was abruptly cancelled. Disappointed and with nothing to do, he drove across the country with thoughts of becoming a writer, or learning to bake bread. He started cooking to support himself and eventually landed in the kitchen of Nancy Silverton's La Brea Bakery in Los Angeles, California.

Cooking was clearly Barber's direction at this point. He returned to New York and entered the French Culinary Institute, graduating in 1994. He then moved to Paris, where he connected with Michel Rostang, an acclaimed third-generation French chef with two Michelin stars now. Barber says that the things he learned in Paris—besides how to survive long, grueling hours—were discipline, technique, and the importance of sourcing good ingredients. Rostang subsequently helped him find work at several restaurants in the south of France.

Returning to New York after a year in France, Barber was hired by David Bouley, who once told him, "When your back is not against the wall, you'll never really create something brilliant." Whereas a lot of people like the freedom to create, Bouley loves "chaos and extreme environments" to produce his artistic dishes, Barber notes. "He called it 'kicking the ball around,' which is putting yourself on the line with new ideas and flavor combinations, and that's how you learn, and that's how you come up with these things under great pressure."

Barber started his own part-time catering operation with his brother David, and landed a job as executive chef at a French restaurant called La Cigale in Manhattan's Lower East Side. He had never been interested in opening a restaurant, but he was hooked on cooking. When he and his brother needed space for a new and larger kitchen for the catering business, they found it in Greenwich Village. "We sort of moved the catering business into the kitchen and realized that it was the perfect place for a restaurant, a small restaurant. We could do both the catering and the restaurant. And that's how it started. I hired a chef and kind of kept the menu and the catering menu similar. It worked for a little while, and the restaurant became quite busy. I became less enamored of the catering. And that was that," says Barber. He felt that he had more control over the food

in a restaurant setting than as a caterer, and eventually, the business evolved into Blue Hill restaurant, named after the family farm.

It didn't take long for Barber to make a name for himself. In the summer of 2002, two years after Blue Hill opened, *Food & Wine* featured Barber as one of the country's "Best New Chefs."

During the first year of Blue Hill, the Barbers were invited to submit a proposal to lease a restaurant to be housed in a converted dairy barn owned by the Rockefeller family in Pocantico Hills, New York. More established chefs were also approached. The Barbers won the bid, however. As Barber says, "We had good qualifications, and we had also established some special relationships with farmers in the Hudson Valley that went beyond the Greenmarket."

The project, which initially granted them restaurant space, began to evolve into a new and dynamic agricultural project, Stone Barns Center for Food and Agriculture. Blue Hill at Stone Barns opened alongside Stone Barns Center in 2004. Hewing closely to his ideals, Barber cooks with meat, poultry, herbs, and vegetables raised and grown at Stone Barns, from nearby farms, and from his family's Blue Hill Farm. Seedlings are grown in Stone Barns Center's 23,000-square-foot soil-to-soil indoor greenhouse.

Also board member of Stone Barns Center, Barber lectures, writes, and works to educate people about how good farming practices relate to the quality of food on dinner tables. Barber continues to build a reputation as one of the country's leading and most outspoken advocates of changing the way food is produced so that healthy, good food remains on the dinner table in the future.

The diversity of what's available, in terms of the types of vegetables and breeds of animals, has significantly declined, even during the ten years he has been in business, he says. If chefs do not involve themselves with farmers, then they will have to rely on distributors and other middlemen in the food production chain. "Unless we are dealing directly with a farmer on the kinds of things that we want and having these kind of in-depth conversations about what we need, we are going to face a world with a lot of diminished flavors and a lot of diminished offerings. We can't afford that," he states.

The time has come, he says, for chefs to "not look back at the nostalgic farmer-chef relationship, but to look forward to embrace a different kind of relationship that's much more involved and technologically driven and passionate—in a way that we are passionate about what goes on from the moment those products arrive in the kitchen."

Barber's overriding message is that the challenge ahead is to produce nutritious food with flavor at an affordable cost with wise agricultural practices. "This sounds ridiculously axiomatic, but I'll say it anyway," he emphasizes.

"THERE'S NO SUCH THING AS A GOOD-TASTING CARROT THAT DOESN'T HAVE BEHIND IT GOOD ECOLOGY AND GOOD SOIL STRUCTURE THAT IT WAS GROWN IN. USUALLY, IT HAS A GOOD COMMUNITY THAT'S SUPPORTING IT TOO.

Beautiful delicious leg of lamb—it's not done by some kind of miracle. It's done because the lamb ate good grass, and because it had the right breed, the right farmer, and the right decisions were made to get it to you that way."

Barber thinks that the food choices that people make are tied to "political realities. Whether it is buying for the family or eating out, they send messages that connect to the economy, ecology, nutrition, and the environment and a whole host of issues that are impossible to separate from how we eat."

Reflecting on what it takes to be a good chef in today's world, Barber says that one must be prepared to sacrifice and work what seems like "insurmountable or unconscionable hours" and embrace the labor. Sacrifice is inevitable in all professions, he says, adding, "I think all chefs would argue that you sacrifice more being a chef. And I just believe—and I think most chefs would believe—that to be a really committed, devoted, hardworking chef, especially in New York City, you have to sacrifice a lot."

And that, he says, is not a lament or a complaint.

GREENHOUSE SALAD *with* BLUE HILL FARM YOGURT

BLUE HILL FARM YOGURT

¾ cup whole milk

¼ cup heavy cream

2 tablespoons plain yogurt

PICKLED FORONO BEETS

6 tablespoons sugar

2 tablespoons kosher salt

1 cup champagne vinegar

1 cup rice vinegar

2 Forono beets, peeled and
shaved on a mandoline

PISTOU

2 cups (packed) fresh basil leaves

Kosher salt

½ cup thinly sliced peeled carrots

2 cups small broccoli florets (about 6 ounces)

1 cup small cauliflower florets (4 to 5 ounces)

1 cup vegetable stock or broth

½ cup cooked cranberry beans or
other winter shelling beans

½ cup (packed) fresh Italian parsley leaves

¼ cup extra-virgin olive oil

Freshly ground black pepper

SALAD

2 small carrots, thinly shaved

6 baby turnips, thinly shaved

Kosher salt

Freshly ground black pepper

White balsamic vinegar

3 cups mixed foraged greens and shoots
(or whatever is fresh at your farmers' market)

1 cup mixed fresh herbs, such as parsley,
tarragon, chervil, thyme, mint, chives

To make the yogurt

1. In a small pot, bring the milk and cream to a boil. Cool the mixture to 109.4°F/43°C and whisk in the yogurt. Transfer the contents to a sterilized jar and place it in a thermal circulator for 12 to 14 hours at 109.4°F/43°C.

2. When the yogurt is thick, strain it. Line a strainer with cheesecloth and set it over a bowl. Place the yogurt in the strainer, and refrigerate for at least 2 hours; preferably overnight.

CONTINUED

To make the pickled beets

1. In a small nonreactive saucepan, bring the sugar, salt, champagne vinegar, rice vinegar, and 2 cups water to a boil, stirring to dissolve the sugar. Remove from the heat and let cool. Add the beets to a nonreactive bowl and pour the liquid over. Cover and refrigerate until ready to use.

To make the pistou

1. Bring a large saucepan of water to a boil. Prepare an ice water bath. Add the basil to the boiling water and simmer for 15 seconds. Using a strainer or slotted spoon, transfer the basil directly to a blender. Add 1 teaspoon of the salt to the water and return it to a boil. Add the carrots and cook 5 minutes. Add the broccoli and cauliflower, and cook until all the vegetables are tender, about 5 minutes longer. Drain. Using a slotted spoon, transfer the vegetables to the ice water and let stand until cold. Drain well. Add the vegetables, stock, beans, and parsley to the blender. With the motor running, add the oil and purée until smooth, occasionally scraping down the sides of the blender with a rubber spatula. Season with salt and pepper.

To make the salad

1. In a bowl, combine the shaved carrots and turnips. Season with salt and pepper and drizzle with white balsamic vinegar to taste. Remove the pickled beets from their brine.

2. In a large bowl, toss together the greens, herbs, beets, carrots, and turnips. Season with salt and pepper.

3. To serve, using a large spoon, spread streaks of pistou and yogurt on serving plates. Top with the greens mixture.

SERVES 6

 **ZUCCHINI**

16 very thin slices pancetta

16 baby zucchinis, with blossoms attached

1 large egg

1½ cups sesame seeds

Vegetable oil, for deep-frying

Salt

Freshly ground black pepper

1. Preheat the oven to 350°F.

2. Wrap 1 pancetta slice around each zucchini, covering most of the zucchini.

3. Whisk the egg in a medium bowl. Put the sesame seeds in another medium bowl.

4. Dip each pancetta-wrapped zucchini into the beaten egg to coat, then into the sesame seeds, turning to coat it generously on all sides. Place the coated zucchini on a baking sheet lined with waxed paper.

5. Pour the oil into a medium saucepan to a depth of 2 inches. Attach a deep-fry thermometer to the side of the pan and heat the oil to 350°F. Working in batches, fry the zucchini until the sesame seeds are golden, about 1 minute. Transfer the zucchini to paper towels to drain.

6. Arrange the zucchini on a baking sheet and bake until they begin to soften, about 7 minutes. Sprinkle generously with salt and pepper.

SERVES 16

2010

TOM COLICCHIO

CHAPTER *twenty-one*

PLEASE DO NOT LABEL TOM COLICCHIO A CELEBRITY CHEF. HE'LL OBJECT. "BRAD PITT ISN'T CALLED A CELEBRITY ACTOR," HE POINTS OUT. "I'M NOT A CELEBRITY. I'M A CHEF." That is Colicchio's calling, and he is content, comfortable, and successful in his role as chef and the conjurer behind the magic of the Craft group of restaurants.

He's also husband and father, son and brother, child-hunger activist, guitar collector, and a saltwater fly fisherman. At the same time, he's head judge on Bravo's hit reality cooking series *Top Chef*. Being voted one of the "Sexiest Men Alive" by *People* magazine, along with Brad Pitt, just makes him laugh. Colicchio laughs about rock-star chefs. "Let me tell you—I know a few rock stars. I've hung out with a few rock stars. Chefs are definitely not rock stars."

Creating a trend wasn't the objective in 2001 when Colicchio left Manhattan's successful Gramercy Tavern, where he was the founding chef and co-owner. Why did he leave behind a sure thing for the risky business of opening a new kind of restaurant? There were some notions about cooking and dining that he wanted to work out. Colicchio's nature is to constantly push forward. There was no reason to change Gramercy Tavern, where he remained for three years after opening Craft. "I'm still proud to have been associated with it. It's a great restaurant," he says.

He opened Craft just a block away. The restaurant is based on creating a dramatic, pared-down version of what Colicchio had spent his career developing. He envisioned simple, good-quality, straightforward dishes that he now calls "contemporary American." Craft, the restaurant, underlines his strong belief that cooking is a craft.

"IT'S NOT ABOUT THE ARTISTRY. IT'S ABOUT CRAFTSMANSHIP. IT'S NOT ABOUT COMBINING INGREDIENTS OR ADDING A BUNCH OF INGREDIENTS. IT'S ABOUT FINDING THE PERFECT SEASONAL INGREDIENT AND ENHANCING IT," COLICCHIO EMPHASIZES.

He realized over time that he had been removing ingredients from recipes. It was a revelation. "As chefs, we each have a repertoire of dishes we carry around like security blankets. When spring comes along, we tend to dust off our spring recipes. When a chef is experienced, and cooking really well, there's a level of confidence. I didn't need the bells and whistles anymore," he says. In Colicchio's kitchen, garnishes and a lot of sauces are unnecessary.

His take on cooking is: "Showcase the product and really showcase what that ingredient is about. Cook it simply and put it on a plate without garnishing it to death, without having five or six components to a dish. That was really how it started. It's fine dining stripped down. It's an evolution. It's always about something I find interesting."

For Colicchio, it's also about challenging himself and figuring out what he feels like doing. As he admits, "It is never about creating a trend or creating a concept. For me, it's always about what do I feel like eating—what do I feel like doing right now in my career?"

His career began with an early interest in food and cooking at home that led to his father's suggestion that Colicchio consider becoming a chef. "It was important to my father that his three sons do something they really loved," he explains. "Success was secondary. I think it was the only time I listened to my dad." One brother became a top international accountant and the other a revered Linden, New Jersey, basketball coach.

Colicchio read everything that he could about cooking, and discovered Jacques Pépin's *La Technique* at home. He remembers, "My dad was a corrections officer, so it may have come from the jail library. In the last paragraph of the introduction, it reads, 'Don't look at this as a cookbook. Look at this as an apprenticeship.' So, I figured, 'Why do I have to go to culinary school to learn how to cook?'"

He decided he could learn how to cook on the job, so Colicchio worked his way through Pépin's legendary illustrated manual *La Méthode*. At the age of seventeen, he toughed his way through the kitchen at Evelyn's Seafood Restaurant in his hometown, Elizabeth, New Jersey. He eventually followed a traditional culinary training path at various restaurants, including a turn in France. Colicchio worked at the Michelin two-starred Hôtel de France in Auch, Gascony, with the father of Ariane Daguin (owner of D'Artagnan).

By his mid-twenties, Colicchio realized he needed to develop his personal style. "For too long I was just reading books and emulating other chefs' cooking," he says. He didn't have a mentor, partly because he didn't stay at any one restaurant long enough, he says. Strategic about his new targets within New York City, he worked briefly for Alfred Portale at the Gotham Bar and Grill, and then was recruited by the Quilted Giraffe in Manhattan. He ended up working at Rakel with Thomas Keller. "I was there right after they opened up, and I was a sous-chef when I left for Mondrian," Colicchio recalls.

In 1991, as executive chef of Mondrian, *Food & Wine* magazine named him as one of the top ten "Best New Chefs" in the United States, and the *New York Times* gave the restaurant three stars.

Colicchio and partner Danny Meyer opened Gramercy Tavern in 1994, and in 1996, Ruth Reichl of the *New York Times* awarded the restaurant three stars, noting that Colicchio was "cooking with extraordinary confidence, creating dishes characterized by bold flavors and unusual harmonies." His cooking at Gramercy Tavern won major recognition and he earned the James Beard Foundation Award for Best Chef: New York in 2000.

Colicchio opened Craft a year later to praise and another three-star *New York Times* review. He retained his ownership of Gramercy until 2006, when he decided to sell his share to concentrate his efforts on Craft.

Moving ahead at Craft with new ideas that extended to plating and the dining room, Colicchio felt that the idea of sharing food and the action of passing food around a table was missing in restaurants. He wasn't targeting a certain demographic with this concept; he just knew it seemed a natural way to eat. "How do you eat at home?" he asks. "Food is put on the table. You pass it around and everyone helps himself. Family style, on platters, creates the interaction." Aware that some people prefer to be more casual, and others more formal, Craft's dining room has two sides, accommodating different comfort zones.

Colicchio's sense of hospitality comes from a desire to make people happy. "That's what we do in this business," he says.

When Sisha Ortuzar, with whom Colicchio worked at Gramercy Tavern, suggested they open a sandwich place, Colicchio's wife thought up the name 'wichcraft. Rooted in the same food and hospitality philosophies as Craft, 'wichcraft eateries have grown to multiple locations. Ortuzar is a partner in the endeavor, and is executive chef at the latest fine-dining establishment, Riverpark. The Colicchio-Ortuzar relationship is symbiotic. "He has the kitchen. It's his house," Colicchio says. While the menu is Ortuzar's, the style reflects the Colicchio way.

Colicchio's growing restaurant collection has now expanded to include four locations of Craft, two of Craftbar, two of Craftsteak, thirteen of 'wichcraft, and Colicchio & Sons (in the former Craftsteak New York location), named in honor of his three sons. In addition, he is also part owner of Riverpark, also in New York City.

He took a big risk in becoming more entrepreneurial. "We have a lot of young chefs looking for that next position, and if you don't provide the opportunity, they'll go someplace else." Described as a strong leader, fair-minded, loyal, and stubborn, Colicchio's a teddy bear at heart, confides a staff member. He doesn't like the drama of a yelling chef or manager. "Frankly, I don't think it ever works. People shouldn't stand for it," he emphasizes. The success of the Craft restaurant group is due in part to Colicchio's willingness to accept advice from talented and savvy business colleagues to negotiate deals and numbers and keep operations running smoothly. He relied on an experienced backer, Robert Scott, who, before retiring, was the president of Morgan Stanley. Jeffrey Zurofsky and Katie Griecoare are also longtime team members and partners.

When he feels that the business side is taking up too much of his brain, Colicchio steps back and does an occasional "Tom: Tuesday Dinner," presiding in the open kitchen of the private dining room adjacent to Craft, serving a multicourse sampling of the things that he's been considering. As Colicchio puts it, "Half my time, I'm thinking about business, and the other half, I'm thinking about food and different combinations—so the creative side of my brain is working."

He says he didn't get into the business to write books and do television, but they became challenges. "The idea of being a chef is expanding and changing," he says. When Bravo approached him about doing *Top Chef,* he turned it down three times before agreeing to do the show. He had no aspirations of becoming a celebrity. His wife, Lori Silverbush, is an award-winning film producer, so he is aware of what editing can do to a program. Once he signed on as head judge, though, he was astonished by the show's success. When Eric Ripert, chef/owner of Manhattan's Le Bernadin offered to be on the show, and then Alfred Portale was a guest, Colicchio knew it was a hit.

His colleagues are important to him and he maintains close friendships. Colicchio admits, "I'm always excited when someone like Keller or Portale is in my restaurant. The opinion of my peers is very important to me." He jokes about being honored as the James Beard Foundation's 2010 Outstanding Chef. "I don't know how many times they were going to nominate me in this category before they got tired of me," he says. "They finally decided, 'Just give it to him so we can get rid of him.'"

There's a serious side to Colicchio, though. "The power of food goes far beyond our taste buds," he believes. One episode of *Top Chef* during the 2009 season focused on demonstrating to kids the importance of food and healthy cooking. Colicchio feels it's imperative to raise the public's awareness of the fact that many children do not have access to regular, nutritious meals. His mother's work with school lunch programs made an indelible impression, so he's knowledgeable about the link between healthy, well-nourished children and school work. "Even if it is only one good, healthy meal a day at school, we must be committed to providing that, as a minimum. Many schools are putting out food that has had all of the nutrition processed out of it," he says.

Colicchio was an executive producer and Silverbrush was one of the directors and producers of *Hungry in America*, a documentary film that takes a hard look at why one in six Americans is a hungry adult, and why one in four is a hungry child. Colicchio feels so strongly about the subject that he testified on the issue before the U.S. House of Representatives in 2010. "In particular, eradicating child hunger is a personal passion of mine—to help make a difference toward this cause," he says. His restaurants give back to the community by supporting charities including Children of Bellevue, City Meals On Wheels, City Harvest, the Food Bank for New York City, and GrowNYC.

Colicchio has been honored five times by the James Beard Foundation, and has written three cookbooks. The first, *Think Like a Chef* (2000) won the James Beard Foundation Cookbook General Award in 2001. His second cookbook is *Craft of Cooking* (2003). The third is a sandwich book, *'wichcraft: Craft a Sandwich into a Meal—and a Meal into a Sandwich* (2009), each published by Clarkson Potter/Publishers. But awards, accolades, and media exposure, while gratifying, are not the most important things in his life.

"You start having children at a late age and you start thinking of legacy. You start thinking about how you want to be known," the chef explains. "Someone asked me last year, 'How do you want to be known? Do you want to be known as a chef? A restaurateur? As a TV guy?' And I don't want to be known as a TV guy. I'm a chef and restaurateur. So it just got me thinking." He's working hard to capture personal time with his family, and for himself. Colicchio named one of his restaurants Colicchio & Sons, but he doesn't expect his three sons to follow in his footsteps, unless it's out of a love for the business. "I'm just like my father in that regard. I just want them to be happy in what they are doing." He's happy doing exactly what his father had wished for him.

SEA URCHIN *and* CRAB FONDUE

POTATO PURÉE

Salt

2 medium Yukon Gold potatoes

¼ cup heavy cream

½ cup butter

Freshly ground black pepper

SEA URCHIN AND CRAB FONDUE

¾ cup plus 1 tablespoon butter, softened

2 shallots, minced

¼ cup white wine

12 ounces lump crabmeat

16 sea urchin tongues

2 tomatoes, peeled, seeded, and cut in ¼-inch dice

¼ cup minced fresh chives

2 teaspoons fresh lemon juice, plus extra for garnish

Pinch curry powder

Chopped fresh chives, for garnish

To make the potato purée

1. In a medium saucepan over high heat, bring salted water to a boil. Add the potatoes and boil until tender, 20 to 25 minutes. Peel the potatoes and transfer to a food processor or blender. Add the cream and butter and purée until smooth. Season with salt and pepper. Reserve and keep warm.

To make the fondue

1. In a small saucepan over medium heat, bring 1 cup of water to a simmer. Whisk ¾ cup of the butter into the saucepan, 1 tablespoon at a time. Reserve and keep warm.

2. To a medium saucepan over low heat, add the remaining 1 tablespoon butter, warming until it slides across the pan. Add the shallots and cook until they are soft and translucent. Add the wine and reduce by half. Whisk in the reserved butter mixture. Add the crabmeat and sea urchin, stirring continuously until warm. Add the tomatoes, chives, and lemon juice. Season with salt and pepper.

To plate

1. Divide the potato purée among four bowls. Spoon ¼ cup sea urchin–crab mixture over the potato purée in each bowl. Garnish with lemon juice, curry, salt, pepper, and chives.

SERVES 4

SPICE-ROASTED LOBSTER *with* BUTTERMILK CHUTNEY

LOBSTER SPICE MIXTURE

½ teaspoon mustard seeds

½ teaspoon coriander seeds

½ teaspoon fennel seeds

1 bay leaf, crumbled

Pinch cayenne pepper

CANDIED GINGER

2 large knobs (about 4 ounces) fresh ginger, julienned

2 cups simple syrup

Kosher salt

Freshly ground black pepper

CHUTNEY

1 tablespoon olive oil

6 small leeks, white parts only, finely diced

4 scallions, white parts only, sliced on the bias

1 jalapeño pepper, seeded and finely diced

1 teaspoon crushed pink peppercorns

½ teaspoon coriander seeds

½ teaspoon fennel seeds

1½ cups buttermilk

LOBSTER

4 lobster tails, 12 ounces each

1 tablespoon extra-virgin olive oil

4 shelled, uncooked lobster claws

1 teaspoon Lobster Spice

4 tablespoons butter

2 bay leaves

GARNISHES

Mustard microgreens

4 bay leaves

To make the lobster spice mixture

1. In a small skillet or sauté pan over medium-low heat, toast the mustard, coriander, and fennel seeds until fragrant. Transfer the toasted spices to a grinder or mortar. Add the bay leaf and cayenne. Grind and reserve.

To make the candied ginger

1. To a small saucepan over medium-low heat, add the ginger. Cover with the simple syrup and season with salt and pepper. Simmer gently until the ginger becomes translucent, about 20 minutes. Remove from the heat, cool slightly, and drain the contents of the saucepan. Set the ginger aside.

CONTINUED

To make the buttermilk chutney

1. In a medium saucepan over medium-low heat, warm the oil. Add the leeks, scallions, jalapeño, peppercorns, coriander, and fennel. Sweat until tender, without browning, 2 to 3 minutes. Remove from the heat and let cool. Add the buttermilk. Reserve.

To make the lobster

1. Prepare an ice water bath. Wrap each lobster tail in a double layer of plastic wrap. Place a large stockpot on the stove. Add the lobsters and set a heavy ceramic plate atop the tails to hold them in place. Add water and bring it to a boil. Cover and boil for 4 minutes. Remove the tails with a slotted spoon, immediately immersing them in the ice water. Remove the plastic wrap. Remove the meat from the shells and discard the tail vein.

2. Heat the oil in a large skillet over medium-high heat until it shimmers but does not smoke. Sprinkle the lobster tail meat and claws with salt and the lobster spice and add to the skillet. Cook for 30 seconds, then add 2 tablespoons of the butter. Turn the lobster, cook 30 seconds longer, and reduce the heat to low. Add the remaining 2 tablespoons butter and the bay leaves. Cook, turning the lobster in the butter until the meat is just firm, about 1 minute. Remove from the skillet.

To plate

1. Divide the buttermilk chutney among four plates, top each with a lobster tail and a lobster claw. Garnish with candied ginger, the mustard microgreens, and a bay leaf. Serve at room temperature.

SERVES 4

recipe credits

PIZZA WITH SMOKED SALMON AND CAVIAR

From *The Wolfgang Puck Cookbook* by Wolfgang Puck. Copyright © 1986 by Wolfgang Puck. Used by permission of Random House, Inc.

KAISERSCHMARRN

From *Live, Love, Eat!* by Wolfgang Puck. Copyright © 2002 by Wolfgang Puck Worldwide, Inc. Used by permission of Random House, Inc.

SUMMER SALAD (Garden Lettuce Salad)

From *The Art of Simple Food* by Alice Waters. Copyright © 2007 by Alice Waters. Illustrations copyright © 2007 by Patricia Curtan. Used by permission of Clarkson Potter/Publishers, an imprint of the Crown Publishing Group, a division of Random House, Inc.

GREEN HERB CEVICHE WITH CUCUMBER (*Ceviche Verde con Pepino*)

From *Fiesta at Rick's: Fabulous Food for Great Times with Friends* by Rick Bayless and Deann Groen Bayless. Copyright © 2010 by Rick Bayless and Deann Groen Bayless. Used by permission of W. W. Norton & Company, Inc.

SMOKY PEANUT MOLE WITH GRILLED QUAIL (*Codornices Asadas en Mole de Cacahuate*)

From *Rick Bayless's Mexican Kitchen* by Rick Bayless. Copyright © 1996 by Richard Lane Bayless. Reprinted with the permission of Scribner, a division of Simon & Schuster, Inc. All rights reserved.

BRIOCHE (from Caviar with Brioche and Avocado Mousse)

Excerpted from *The French Laundry Cookbook* by Thomas Keller. Copyright © 1999 by Thomas Keller. Used by permission of Artisan, a division of Workman Publishing Co., Inc., New York. All rights reserved.

PACCHERI WITH ANNA SANTORO'S PESTO TRAPANESE (*Paccheri al Pesto Trapanese di Anna Santoro*)

LIMONCELLO TIRAMISÙ

From *Lidia's Italy* by Lidia Matticchio Bastianich and Tanya Bastianich Manuali. Copyright © 2007 by Tutti a Tavola, LLC. Used by permission of Alfred A. Knopf, a division of Random House, Inc.

SPICY CALAMARI (*Calamari Piccanti*)

From *Lidia Cooks from the Heart of Italy* by Lidia Matticchio Bastianich and Tanya Bastianich Manuali with David Nussbaum. Copyright © 2009 by Tutti a Tavola, LLC. Used by permission of Alfred A. Knopf, a division of Random House, Inc.

GRILLED GUINEA HEN WITH FREGULA AND BLACK TRUFFLE VINAIGRETTE

From *The Babbo Cookbook* by Mario Batali. Copyright © 2002 by Mario Batali. Photographs copyright © 2002 by Christopher Hirsheimer. Used by permission of Clarkson Potter/Publishers, an imprint of the Crown Publishing Group, a division of Random House, Inc.

BEET SALAD WITH FETA, ORANGE, AND MINT

From *Alfred Portale Simple Pleasures* by Alfred Portale and Andrew Friedman. Copyright © 2004 by Alfred Portale. Reprinted by permission of Harper Collins Publishers.

acknowledgments

THE PUBLISHER WOULD LIKE TO THANK *Susan Friedland*
FOR HER CONTRIBUTION TO THIS BOOK.

The James Beard Foundation honors extraordinary contributions to American food. It is also a privilege to acknowledge these chefs in a beautiful book. Kudos to literary agent Maura Kye-Casella, James Beard Foundation chairman of the board Woodrow W. Campbell, president Susan Ungaro, vice-president Mitchell Davis, and executive assistant to the president Nancy Kull.

Special thanks to Jan Longone, curator, American Culinary History Clements Library at the Univeristy of Michigan for the Jeremiah Tower archives; Francois Dionot, L'Academie de Cuisine; and Len DePas of The Photographer's Gallery; *Food Arts* Magazine; and Susan Delgado with Nicholas Timmons of Double Image Studios; Phyllis Richman and Verveine Palladin each for access to their Jean-Louis Palladin materials and contributions.

Dedicated individuals support these outstanding chefs. These wizards keep everything moving: Mandy Oser, Georgette Farkas, A.J. Schaller, Mylene Benmoussa, Lisa Scott, Bret Csencsitz, Kristine Keefer, Bertram Whitman, chef Devin Knell, Laura Ryan, Lauren Falk, Liz Gunnison, Mel Davis, Adriana Jurado, Chef Michael Rotondo, Rachel Hayden, Tamara Wood, Jen Fite, Christian Seel, executive chef Chris Muller, executive sous chef Adam Plitt, Varun Mehra, Cristina Mueller, David Prior, Maggie Boone, Rochelle Trotter, Nicole Bartelme, chef Gillian Lowe, executive sous chef Stephen Lyons, Irene Hamburger, Pamela Lewy, Alaric Campbell, and Shelly Burgess.

Our talented executive chef and culinary director, the late Robert D. Barker, translated and guided our way through America's most amazing kitchens. Chef Zack Engel, Linda Ellerbee, Rolfe Tessem, Erin and Billy Jones Miller, Grace Bauer, Lanny Thomas, Harrison Tassopoulos, David Spielman, Daniel Zhao, Kim Ranjbar, Mary Caplinger, Christopher Gromek, Eloisa Rivera Zepeda, Marla Romash, Darryl Spearman, Anne Dalfres, Julia Reed, John Pearce, Sue Grafton, Julie Smith, Alix and Paul Rico gave their encouragement freely. Billy, my husband, gets bouquets for his support, patience, and love.

Our heartfelt appreciation to the pros at Chronicle Books: Bill LeBlond, Dawn Yanagihara, Sarah Billingsley, Alice Chau, and Cat Grishaver with their extraordinary design and marketing teams. They brought a cherished vision to beautiful reality.